Daily Evening Devotional For College Students

5-Minute Devotions To Rest, Reflect, And Rise For Stress-Free Studies

Biblical Teachings

Copyright © 2023 by Biblical Teachings – All rights reserved

The content contained within this book may not be reproduced, duplicated, or transmitted without direct written permission from the author or the publisher.

Under no circumstances will any blame or legal responsibility be held against the publisher, or author, for any damages, reparation, or monetary loss due to the information contained within this book, either directly or indirectly.

Legal Notice:

This book is copyright-protected. It is only for personal use. You cannot amend, distribute, sell, use, quote, or paraphrase any part, or the content within this book, without the author or publisher's permission.

Disclaimer Notice:

Please note that the information contained within this document is for educational and entertainment purposes only. All effort has been executed to present accurate, up-to-date, reliable, and complete information. No warranties of any kind are declared or implied. Readers acknowledge that the author is not rendering legal, financial, medical, or professional advice. The content within this book has been derived from various sources. Please consult a licensed professional before attempting any techniques outlined in this book.

By reading this document, the reader agrees that under no circumstances is the author responsible for any losses, direct or indirect, that are incurred due to the use of the information in this document, including, but not limited to, errors, omissions, or inaccuracies.

Contents

Let the Journey Begin...	VII
REFLECTION AND GRATITUDE	1
1. Daily Moments of Gratitude	2
2. Reflecting on Challenges	4
3. Celebrating Personal Wins	6
4. Mindful Presence	8
5. Identifying Positive Patterns	10
6. Embracing Learning Opportunities	12
7. Purposeful Reflection	14
8. Bible Study - The Healing of the Ten Lepers	16
PREPARING FOR TOMORROW	19
9. Setting Clear Intentions	20
10. Evening Routine	22
11. Review and Adjust	24
12. Balancing Priorities	26
13. Visualizing Success	28
14. Limiting Stress	30

15.	Bible Study - The Ten Virgins	32

BIBLICAL STORIES FOR MODERN COLLEGE LIFE — 35

16.	David and Goliath	36
17.	Gideon	38
18.	Trusting God's Provision - Matthew 6:25-34	40
19.	Moses	42
20.	The Serenity Prayer	44
21.	Jonah and the Whale	46
22.	Bible Study - The Story of Paul	48

NAVIGATING NIGHTLIFE — 51

23.	Fun and Responsibility	52
24.	Peer Pressure and Standing Firm	54
25.	Choosing Your Company Wisely	56
26.	Setting Boundaries and Limits	58
27.	The Morning After	60
28.	Bible Study - The Parable of the Prodigal Son	62

SELF-CARE — 65

29.	Caring for the Temple	66
30.	Sabbath Rest and Sleep Hygiene	68
31.	Creative Exploration	71
32.	Evening Exercise	74
33.	Overcoming Regret	77
34.	Inner Peace	79

35.	Bible Study - Mary and Martha	81
	CONNECTING WITH GOD	84
36.	Prayerful Reflection	85
37.	Creating a Sacred Space	87
38.	Listening in Silence	89
39.	The Examen Prayer	91
40.	Bible Study - Elijah on Mount Horeb	94
	REFLECTING ON RELATIONSHIPS	97
41.	Investing in Friendships	98
42.	Small Acts of Kindness	101
43.	Navigating Conflict	103
44.	Embracing Diversity	106
45.	Active Listening	108
46.	Digital Connections	110
47.	Remembering Christ's Love	113
48.	Bible Study - Learning from Jonathan and David	115
	DIGITAL DETOX	118
49.	Digital Detox	119
50.	Resisting the Fear Of Missing Out (FOMO)	121
51.	Mindful Screen Consumption	123
52.	Rediscovering Face-to-Face Interaction	125
53.	Analog Hobbies	127
54.	Success Story	129

55. Bible Study - Restoring the Temple	132
DREAMS AND ASPIRATIONS	135
56. God's Unique Plan	136
57. Chasing Your Dreams	138
58. Facing Setbacks	140
59. Fear of Failure	142
60. Perseverance and Patience	145
61. Legacy and Impact	148
62. Bible Study - Joseph: From Dreamer to Ruler	151
The Afterword	154

LET THE JOURNEY BEGIN...

College—the pinnacle of youth and adventure, where countless memories are made and dreams are forged. It's an exhilarating chapter of life filled with intense growth, new experiences, and the embrace of endless possibilities. But let's not forget, it can also be one of the most challenging periods you'll ever face.

As I reflect on my own college years, I realize they were far from perfect. Like many of us, I stumbled and made my fair share of mistakes. Yet, it is precisely these missteps that have shaped my understanding and propelled me to share my experiences with you. In the pages that follow, I offer you invaluable insights and lessons, drawing from both triumphs and trials, to help you navigate your own college journey with greater wisdom and grace.

Let me be clear—there's no magic formula to avoid every misstep or guarantee a flawless path. Mistakes are inevitable and often the catalysts for our most profound growth. However, my intention is to equip you with the tools, perspectives, and guidance necessary to make informed choices and maximize your college experience.

Within these pages you'll delve into the world of reflection and gratitude, discover the magic of evening routines, and draw inspiration from timeless biblical stories tailored to your modern college life. We'll explore the vibrant landscape of college nightlife, nurture your well-being with self-care, and deepen your spiritual connection with God. And yes, we will unravel the mysteries of relationships, digital detoxes, and chasing your dreams relentlessly while aligning yourself with God's will. With each turn of the page, you'll unlock avenues for personal and spiritual growth in this chapter of your life.

Together, we'll navigate the maze of reflection and gratitude, evening routines, nightlife, self-care, prayer, digital detox, dreams, aspirations and more, ensuring that your time in college is marked by both personal and spiritual growth.

As you embark on this transformative journey, I invite you to open your heart and mind to the experiences of others. Approach each chapter with a hunger for knowledge, a desire to learn, and an openness to the possibilities that lie ahead. Together, we will navigate the intricacies of college life, armed with the wisdom and insights of those who have walked this path before us.

So, if you're ready to seize every opportunity, make informed decisions, and embrace the adventure that college presents, then this book is your faithful companion. Let it serve as your compass, guiding you through the challenges, triumphs, and discoveries that await. By the time you turn the final page, you'll be equipped with the knowledge and resilience to thrive academically, socially, and spiritually, not just during your college years, but for a lifetime.

Remember, life is indeed a balancing act, and if you can conquer it during your college experience, you'll set yourself up for a future of endless possibilities.

Your journey starts now...

REFLECTION AND GRATITUDE

1

DAILY MOMENTS OF GRATITUDE

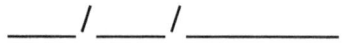

"Give thanks in all circumstances; for this is God's will for you in Christ Jesus."

- 1 THESSALONIANS 5:18

I remember those late nights in the dorm room, the bustling cafeteria, and the rush of classes. College can be a roller coaster, right? But guess what? Amid the chaos, we can find something beautiful – gratitude.

You know, I used to breeze through my days without pausing to appreciate the little things. Until one day, a good friend shared a simple habit – writing three things I'm grateful for each evening. I gave it a try, skeptically. But wow, it certainly influenced my life!

After a long day of lectures, assignments, and maybe even a coffee spill in the library, I could focus on the negatives and how stressful it all was. But instead, I'd sit down and think. What stood out? What was I grateful for that day? Maybe it was that sunny moment between classes or the laughter during lunch. Perhaps it was the roof over my head or something tasty I had for lunch. Suddenly, I realized how many blessings were sprinkled through even the toughest days.

Life at college isn't all about the A's or the parties. It's about growth, connections, and the little moments. Taking a few minutes each night to reflect and find gratitude shifts our mindset. It helps us see beyond the struggles and appreciate the blessings – even the tiniest ones. And trust me, it's these moments that weave into the incredible tapestry of your college journey.

P.S. If you keep your daily gratitude moments in a journal, you can look back at what you've previously been grateful for if you're having a bad day and struggling to think of anything!

Reflection: *What are 3 things you're grateful for today? Try to think of something that made you smile, even for a moment.*

How did gratitude change your perspective today, if at all?

Let us pray... Dear God, as I reflect on this day, I'm reminded of your constant presence. Thank you for the little joys, the shared laughter, and even the challenges that help me grow. Help me find gratitude in each moment, knowing that your blessings are always around me. Amen.

2

REFLECTING ON CHALLENGES

____ / ____ / _____

"Consider it pure joy, my brothers and sisters, whenever you face trials of many kinds, because you know that the testing of your faith produces perseverance."

— JAMES 1:2-3

College can throw curveballs our way, making us feel like we're in a constant challenge marathon. But guess what? Challenges aren't just roadblocks; they're opportunities in disguise.

Picture this: I was working on a group project that seemed impossible to crack. Tight deadlines, clashing schedules – it was a mess. Frustration was knocking on my door, but then I remembered this verse from James. It hit me – every challenge is a chance to grow, to become stronger.

You see, challenges test our limits. They force us to think creatively, collaborate, and persevere. It's like a weight room for our character, making us spiritually and mentally stronger. So, the next time a challenge hits you, don't dread it – embrace it.

Remember, college isn't just about acing exams; it's about acing life's tests. Each challenge is an opportunity to build resilience and character. Reframe your challenges as stepping stones rather than stumbling blocks. Trust me, it's these challenges that shape us into capable men, ready to take on the world.

Reflection: *What challenges have you faced recently? How did they make you feel?*

Can you see any silver lining in these challenges? What are the lessons you're learning?

Let us pray... Dear God, As I face challenges on this college journey, I ask for your wisdom and strength. Help me see beyond the struggle and understand the lessons each challenge brings. Thank you for the growth that comes from overcoming obstacles. Amen.

3

CELEBRATING PERSONAL WINS

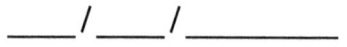

"Do not despise these small beginnings, for the Lord rejoices to see the work begin..."

- ZECHARIAH 4:10

Let's dive into something awesome – celebrating personal wins. We're not talking about big, flashy stuff here. Nope, we're talking about the small victories that are like secret high-fives you give yourself.

Imagine this: You're juggling classes, assignments, and maybe even a part-time job. One day, in the middle of all that chaos, you finally cracked a challenging problem that had you scratching your head for days. It might seem like a drop in the ocean, but it's a big deal! It's like winning a mini trophy on your path.

So, why celebrate these tiny victories? Well, they're like the breadcrumbs that lead you to success. Taking a moment to acknowledge them, even if they seem small, helps you stay motivated and grateful. It's like giving your future self a pat on the back.

Here's the deal: College life can be a rollercoaster. There will be days when you'll feel like you're stuck in a whirlwind. In moments like these, recognizing and celebrating your small victories brings a ray of sunshine. It keeps you moving forward, step by step.

Reflection: *Have you ever brushed off a small victory thinking it wasn't worth celebrating? How could celebrating it impact your outlook?*

Can you plan a way to acknowledge your small wins regularly? Consider how this might help boost your motivation and gratitude.

Let us pray... Dear God, thank you for the little triumphs that brighten my college journey. Help me to notice and celebrate them, knowing that You take joy in my progress. Guide me to embrace these moments, no matter how small, and use them to keep moving forward. Amen.

4

MINDFUL PRESENCE

___ / ___ / _____

> *"Do not be anxious about anything, but in every situation, by prayer and petition, with thanksgiving, present your requests to God. And the peace of God, which transcends all understanding, will guard your hearts and your minds in Christ Jesus."*
>
> – PHILIPPIANS 4:6-7 (NIV)

Today, I want to share something that helped me not just survive, but thrive during my college years: mindful presence.

You see, college life can be overwhelming. The constant rush from one class to another, the pressure of assignments, and the anticipation of what's to come after graduation can consume us. I've been there, lost in thought, worrying about the future while missing out on the beauty of the present moment.

One day, I stumbled upon Philippians 4:6-7, and it hit me like a ton of bricks. It says not to be anxious but to present our requests to God with thanksgiving. This verse isn't just about prayer; it's also about being present and mindful. It's a call to focus on what's happening right now, without letting anxiety steal our joy.

So, here's what I did and encourage you to do too: I started paying attention to the little things around me. The rustling of leaves in the wind, the warmth of the sun on my face, or the laughter of friends during a study break. I began to practice gratitude for the present moment.

Reflection: *What are some things in your daily college life that you often overlook because you're too busy thinking about the future?*

How can practicing mindfulness and gratitude help reduce anxiety and stress in your college journey?

Have you ever experienced a moment of mindful presence where you felt truly alive and at peace? What was it?

Let us pray... Dear God, thank you for the gift of the present moment. Help me to be mindful and present, appreciating the beauty and opportunities that surrounds me. When anxiety and worry creep in, remind me to turn to you in prayer and with thanks. May your peace guard my hearts and minds as I navigate this season of life. Amen.

5

IDENTIFYING POSITIVE PATTERNS

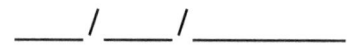

"In all your ways submit to him, and he will make your paths straight."

– PROVERBS 3:6 (NIV)

Have you ever sat back and tried to identify positive patterns within your life? If you're sat there wondering what I'm talking about, let me explain.

When I was in college, I noticed something crucial. I began to see patterns in my daily life—the routines, habits, and choices that defined who I was becoming. Some of these patterns were positive, like setting aside time for prayer, staying disciplined in my studies, and building strong friendships.

But I also observed negative patterns. Procrastination, late-night binging on junk food, and neglecting my spiritual growth were among them. I realized that if I didn't take charge of these patterns, they would shape my college experience and, ultimately, my future.

That's when I turned to Proverbs 3:6. It says to submit all your ways to God, and He will make your paths straight. It's a reminder that we can choose the patterns we want to follow and let God guide us toward the right ones.

So, my challenge for you today is this: take a moment to reflect on the patterns and habits you've noticed in your college journey. Identify the positive ones you want to nurture and the negative ones you want to change.

Reflection: *What positive patterns have you established, or want to, in your college life that have contributed to your well-being and growth?*

Are there any negative patterns or habits you've noticed that hinder your progress or happiness? How can you work on changing them?

How can submitting your ways to God help you navigate college life and make your path straight?

Let us pray... Dear God, thank you for guiding me through our college journey. Help me to recognize the patterns and habits in my life and to choose those that align with your will. Give me the strength and wisdom to change the negative patterns and cultivate positive ones. May my path be straight as I submit to you. Amen.

6

EMBRACING LEARNING OPPORTUNITIES

____ / ____ / _____

"The heart of the discerning acquires knowledge, for the ears of the wise seek it out."

– PROVERBS 18:15 (NIV)

The ability to spot, and embrace, learning opportunities is one the most beneficial skills you can possibly have.

In college, the learning never stops. I'm not just talking about academically. Each day, you encounter new information, ideas, and perspectives in many areas of life. It's easy to get caught up in the hustle and bustle, but I encourage you to pause and reflect on these moments of discovery.

Proverbs 18:15 reminds us that the heart of the discerning acquires knowledge. In other words, wise individuals actively seek out opportunities to learn. It's not just about what you're taught in the classroom but also what you learn outside of it.

Think about it—maybe today you had a thought-provoking discussion with a friend, stumbled upon an interesting article, learned about new side-hustle, heard a speaker who challenged your beliefs, or figured out how to improve a skill. These are all learning opportunities.

So, embrace these moments of growth. Seek knowledge and wisdom in every experience, whether big or small, and incorporate these learning opportunities into your own personal growth journey.

Reflection: *Can you recall a specific moment today when you encountered new information or ideas? What was it, and how did it impact you?*

How can you actively seek out opportunities to learn, both inside and outside the classroom, during your college experience?

In what ways can embracing learning opportunities contribute to your personal growth and development as a Christian college student?

Let us pray... Dear God, thank you for the gift of knowledge and the opportunities to learn and grow. Help me to have a discerning heart and seek wisdom in every experience I encounter during my college journey. May I have the confidence to embrace these learning opportunities and use them to become wiser and more faithful. Amen.

7

PURPOSEFUL REFLECTION

____/____/_____

"Your word is a lamp for my feet, a light on my path."

– PSALM 119:105 (NIV)

Psalm 119:105 tells us that God's Word is a light on our path. Even though we have no idea where life will take us, we don't need to worry because God's Word will guide us safely forward. When we reflect, it's like turning on a light in the darkness. When you take time to think about your day, your experiences, and your actions, you gain insights that can guide you on the right path.

Here's an example. Perhaps you had a particularly challenging day. Classes seemed overwhelming, and you argued with friends. In the midst of it all, you may feel like everything is against you.

But when you sit down to reflect, you start to see things more clearly. Maybe you realize that you could have handled a situation with more patience or that you need to manage your time more effectively. Reflection helps you uncover those moments of growth and learning so you can move forward and avoid those scenarios in the future.

Each day, take time to think about what you've experienced and what you've learned. If you do, you'll be turning on that lamp to illuminate your path toward personal growth and a deeper relationship with God.

Reflection: *What was a significant event or moment from today that you can reflect on? What did you learn from it?*

How do you think purposeful reflection help you make better decisions and grow as a college student, an adult, and a Christian?

Moving forward, how can you incorporate a regular practice of reflecting on your day, whether through journaling, prayer, or quiet contemplation?

Let us pray... Dear God, thank you for your guidance and wisdom. Help me to cultivate the habit of purposeful reflection in my life. May your Word be a lamp for my feet, lighting my path toward personal growth and a deeper relationship with you. Amen.

8

BIBLE STUDY - THE HEALING OF THE TEN LEPERS

Luke 17:11-19

The story of the ten lepers from Luke 17:11-19 is a powerful reminder of the importance of gratitude and reflection in our lives. In this story, Jesus heals ten lepers, but only one returns to express his gratitude. This Bible study will explore how we can celebrate our personal wins, reflect on challenges, and practice gratitude, just as the thankful leper did, in our college journey.

Reading: First, read the passage from Luke 17:11-19 to understand the story of the ten lepers.

Discussion:

1. **Recognizing Blessings**: In the story, only one leper returned to thank Jesus for his healing. How can we become more attuned to recognizing and acknowledging the blessings and miracles in our own lives?

2. **Personal Wins**: Celebrating personal wins can boost our morale and motivation. Share a recent personal win or achievement, whether big or small, and explain how it made you feel.

3. **Overcoming Challenges**: Reflect on a recent challenge or setback you faced. How did you overcome it, and what lessons did you learn from the experience?

4. **Gratitude Practice**: The act of expressing gratitude has a profound impact on our well-being. What daily or weekly practices can you establish to cultivate gratitude in your life?

5. **Reflecting on Growth**: In the story, the leper's gratitude was tied to his healing and transformation. How can we reflect on our personal growth and transformation during our college journey?

6. **Encouraging Thankfulness**: How can we encourage and support our peers to practice thankfulness and express gratitude for the blessings in their lives?

7. **Mindful Living**: How can practicing mindfulness help us become more aware of the present moment, fostering a deeper sense of gratitude and reflection?

Reflection: *Take a moment to reflect on the story of the ten lepers and the importance of gratitude in your college journey. Consider how you can implement gratitude practices, celebrate personal wins, and navigate challenges with a thankful heart.*

Let us pray... Dear God, as we dive into the story of the ten lepers, we are reminded of the transformative power of gratitude and reflection. Help us cultivate thankful hearts, celebrating our personal wins, reflecting on our challenges, and recognizing Your blessings in our college journey. May our lives be a testament to Your grace and love. Amen.

PREPARING FOR TOMORROW

9

SETTING CLEAR INTENTIONS

____/____/_____

"Commit to the Lord whatever you do, and he will establish your plans."

– PROVERBS 16:3 (NIV)

Do you remember the last time you went to bed knowing you didn't have much to do the next day? Each new day is a blank canvas and a new opportunity for us to paint it with our actions and choices.

Today's devotion is about the power of setting clear intentions and how they can transform your life.

Setting clear intentions is like having a roadmap for your day. It empowers you to take the wheel, directing your energy and focus towards your goals.

For instance, if you have a significant test on the horizon, your intention might be to tackle your studies with unwavering determination and unwavering focus. If spiritual growth is your aim, set an intention to spend quality time in prayer and reflection. Perhaps you want to improve your social skills? Try setting an intention to strike up a conversation with someone new each day!

Whether it's acing that challenging exam, nurturing your personal growth, or anything else you have in mind, intentions pave the way.

Reflection: *Recall a time when you set specific intentions for your day. How did it affect your productivity and overall well-being?*

Consider what intentions you can set that will help you for different areas of your life such as academics, personal life, and spiritual growth during your college journey.

Let us pray... Dear God, I'm so grateful for the gift of each new day. Help me to craft clear intentions that align with your divine plan. May my intentions be a source of strength, guiding me towards fulfilling my purpose during my college journey. Amen.

10

EVENING ROUTINE

_____ / _____ / _____

"But everything should be done in a fitting and orderly way."

– 1 Corinthians 14:40 (NIV)

Do you want to know the secret to calmer mornings and more productive days? An evening routine.

Before you roll your eyes, let me set the scene...

You've had a long day full of classes, meetings, assignments, and other commitments, and the night is slowly creeping in. We all know how tempting it is to kick off your clothes at the first sight of bed and jump straight onto Netflix or some video games. But here's a life hack the most successful people use: an evening routine that sets the stage for an amazing day ahead.

1 Corinthians 14:40 reminds us to do everything in a fitting and orderly way. By dedicating a bit of time to prepare for the next day, you can save yourself from the morning rush and stress.

So, let's break it down. Your evening routine might include laying out your clothes for the next day, preparing a simple meal or snack, tidying up mess before it accumulates, organizing your study materials, or going to bed at a similar time each night. These seemingly small tasks can make a world of difference when you're racing against the clock in the morning.

Perhaps you have a morning routine you need to set up for. How about having everything ready so you can jump straight into it once you wake up? This will aid you in staying consistent too!

The lesson here is simple but powerful—an organized evening routine not only makes your mornings smoother but also frees up mental space for you to focus on what truly matters.

Reflection: *What does your current evening routine look like, and how does it affect your mornings and overall college experience?*

Consider the tasks you can incorporate into your evening routine to make your mornings more efficient. What steps can you take to better prepare for the day ahead?

Reflect on how an organized evening routine can contribute to a sense of peace and order in your life, allowing you to approach each day with greater clarity and purpose.

Let us pray... Dear God, thank you for the gift of organization and order. Help me to establish an evening routine that not only eases my mornings but also allows me to approach each day with a sense of calm and purpose. Guide me in making fitting and orderly choices in my daily life. Amen.

11

REVIEW AND ADJUST

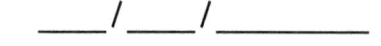

"Many are the plans in a person's heart, but it is the Lord's purpose that prevails."

– PROVERBS 19:21 (NIV)

I'm sure you've noticed, life doesn't always go as planned. In fact, sometimes it feels like your life is constantly shifting like a big tangled knot. But here's the beauty of it—you can still thrive by learning the art of reviewing and adjusting your goals.

Proverbs 19:21 reminds us that while we may have many plans, it's ultimately the Lord's purpose that prevails. This verse speaks to the importance of being adaptable and flexible in our pursuits.

Put yourself in this scenario... you've mapped out a meticulous plan for your day, but suddenly, an unexpected assignment, or a friend in need of help, throws a curveball your way. No matter how much you want to kick and scream, at this point you have a choice to make— either resist the change and become more and more frustrated, or to review and adjust your plans.

The lesson here is that flexibility is a valuable skill, not just in college but throughout life. It's about being willing to adapt when circumstances shift, all while keeping your ultimate purpose and faith in God's guidance in mind.

Reflection: *Think back on a recent day when your plans had to change unexpectedly. How did you react, and what did you learn from that experience?*

Consider the balance between setting goals and being flexible. How can you strike that balance in your college journey?

Reflect on the times when you've had to adapt your plans. Did it lead to unexpected opportunities or growth?

Let us pray... Dear God, grant me the wisdom to set my goals with purpose, but also the humility to adjust when life takes an unexpected turn. Help me trust in your ultimate purpose for my life, knowing that even in the midst of change, you are guiding my steps. Amen.

12

BALANCING PRIORITIES

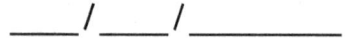

"There is a time for everything, and a season for every activity under the heavens."

– ECCLESIASTES 3:1 (NIV)

Trying to balance everything in life can feel like juggling chainsaws. It's no easy feat, but it's one of the most important skills you can master. It isn't just about managing your academic workload; it's about crafting a harmonious life that encompasses all your responsibilities, dreams, and relationships.

Ecclesiastes 3:1 reminds us that life unfolds in seasons. Just like nature transitions through different seasons, so do our lives. There are times for studying, times for friends and other relationships, times for self-discovery, and times for relaxation.

Prioritizing means recognizing that not all tasks hold the same weight. It means understanding that your energy and focus are finite resources. Therefore, it's crucial to assess what truly matters in the present moment and allocate your time and effort accordingly.

If you had an exam tomorrow, a close friend's birthday party tonight, and a personal project you're deeply passionate about. When you receive the party invitation, you're faced with a decision. How can you prioritize what needs to be done?

You could acknowledge the significance of the exam and your commitment to personal growth. So, you decide to prioritize studying for the exam tonight, attend the party briefly to celebrate with your friend, and then dedicate focused time to your project tomorrow.

That's just one example of many you could face. Life will regularly throw curveballs at you to test you, so you'd better get those priorities straight!

Reflection: *Reflect on a time when you felt overwhelmed by attempting to manage multiple responsibilities simultaneously. How did it affect your well-being and performance?*

Consider the various seasons or priorities in your life at this moment—academics, relationships, personal growth. How can you allocate your time and energy to honor these priorities effectively?

Let us pray... Dear God, please grant me the wisdom to recognize the seasons in my life and the ability to prioritize my responsibilities. Help me balance my academic, social, and personal priorities in a way that aligns with your purpose for me. Guide me in managing my time wisely. Amen.

13

VISUALIZING SUCCESS

_____ / _____ / _____ VISUALIZING SUCCESS

"I can do all this through him who gives me strength."

– PHILIPPIANS 4:13 (NIV)

Let's talk about a superpower that you possess – a power that can elevate your college journey. It's called positive visualization, and it's not some mystical practice; it's a practical tool that can change the way you approach challenges and goals.

Imagine this: You've got a major presentation on the horizon. Your heart races at the mere thought of standing in front of your class, the spotlight on you. Doubts creep in – what if you stumble, what if you forget your words? We've all been there, right?

The pressure can be overwhelming, but here's a secret weapon I learned for when self-doubt reared it's ugly head – positive visualization.

Philippians 4:13 reminds us that we can do all things through Christ who strengthens us. This verse holds the essence of the lesson I want to share. It's about harnessing the power of your mind to see yourself succeeding, to believe in your abilities, and to draw strength from your faith.

Close your eyes for a moment and visualize yourself confidently walking into that interview room and impressing the interviewers with your skills and experience, easily answering every question on an exam, the feeling of accomplishment, the handshake of approval, and the sense of pride welling up within you.

Positive visualization isn't just daydreaming—it's a powerful mental exercise that can boost your confidence and motivation. When you can see yourself succeeding, it becomes easier to overcome hurdles and reach your goals. With God's strength, you can overcome any challenge that comes your way.

Reflection: *Think about a recent challenge you faced. How did your mindset and self-belief impact the outcome?*

Consider the tasks and challenges you have coming up. How can you incorporate positive visualization to boost your confidence and motivation?

Reflect on how Philippians 4:13 applies to your life. How can you draw strength from your faith to overcome challenges and visualize success?

Let us pray... Dear God, I thank you for the gift of faith and the ability to visualize success. Help me tap into the power of positive thinking and believe in my abilities. Strengthen my confidence and motivation as I face the challenges of college life. Amen.

14

LIMITING STRESS

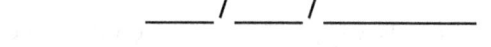

"In peace I will lie down and sleep, for you alone, Lord, make me dwell in safety."

– PSALM 4:8 (NIV)

After a long day, why is it sometimes so hard time to unwind and recharge? It's likely that your mind is still racing with the day's pressures, future deadlines, anxiety, and more.

I know what it's like to stay up all night for a marathon study session. The clock reads 10 PM, and your inner perfectionist is pushing you to keep going. You feel the weight of unfinished work, but you also know that rest is essential for tomorrow's productivity.

In this moment you must make a choice. To keep working, or not to keep working, that is the question.

I solved this issue by setting myself boundaries – a time to stop working and transition peacefully into my evening routine. Your body will begin to recognize this pattern and find it easier to unwind in the evenings. As a by-product I found it also helped me to get more work done as I knew

I needed to wrap up at a certain time.

Remember: Rest is just as crucial as productivity. The last thing you want to do is burn yourself out.

So, as you prepare for the day ahead, remember that managing evening stress is a skill that can positively impact your college experience. By setting boundaries and creating a peaceful transition into the evening, you can find the rest and rejuvenation you need to thrive.

Reflection: *Think about the evening stressors you've encountered recently. How did they affect your ability to relax and recharge?*

Consider the strategies you can implement to set boundaries and create a peaceful evening routine. How can you make the transition from day to night smoother?

Let us pray... Dear God, I thank you for the gift of peace, especially in the midst of college chaos. Help me set boundaries with my work or studies in the evening, allowing for a peaceful transition. Grant me the wisdom to prioritize rest and faith in Your guidance for a restful night's sleep. Amen.

BIBLE STUDY - THE TEN VIRGINS

Matthew 25:1-13

The Parable of the Ten Virgins, found in Matthew 25:1-13, conveys a profound message about preparedness and vigilance. In this parable, Jesus highlights the importance of being ready for unexpected events, much like college men preparing for the challenges and opportunities each new day brings. This Bible study will delve into the parable, helping us explore practical ways to be prepared for the days ahead during our college journey.

Reading: First, read the passage from Matthew 25:1-13 to understand the Parable of the Ten Virgins.

Discussion:

1. **Preparedness and Readiness**: In the parable, some virgins were prepared with oil for their lamps, while others were not. How does this parable remind us of the importance of preparedness and readiness in our daily lives?

2. **Anticipating Challenges**: College life comes with its own set of challenges and opportunities. How can you anticipate and prepare for academic, personal, or spiritual challenges you may encounter?

3. **Setting an Evening Routine**: Discuss the significance of establishing an evening routine that helps you prepare for the following day. What practices can you incorporate into your evening routine to promote readiness?

4. **Vigilance and Alertness**: The virgins had to be vigilant and alert, not knowing when the bridegroom would arrive. How can you maintain a state of vigilance in your college journey, especially regarding your goals and aspirations?

5. **Investing in Spiritual Preparedness**: In the parable, oil symbolizes spiritual preparedness. How can you invest in your spiritual well-being and preparedness for each day as a college student?

6. **Prioritizing Priorities**: The virgins had to prioritize buying oil. What are your academic, personal, and spiritual priorities, and how can you ensure you are allocating your time and resources accordingly?

7. **Supportive Community**: The virgins were part of a group awaiting the bridegroom. How can you build a supportive community of friends and mentors who can help you stay prepared for college challenges?

Reflection: *Reflect on your daily routines and habits. How can the Parable of the Ten Virgins inspire you to establish or enhance your evening routine to better prepare for the days ahead in college?*

Let us pray... Dear God, as we contemplate the Parable of the Ten Virgins, we recognize the importance of preparedness and vigilance in our daily lives. Grant us the wisdom to establish evening routines that promote readiness for the challenges and opportunities of each new day in our college journey. May we be vigilant and prepared, both spiritually and practically, as we await the unfolding of Your plans for us. Amen.

Optional Homework: Create yourself a personalized evening routine that aligns with your academic, personal, and spiritual goals. Share your routine with a trusted friend or mentor for accountability and feedback.

BIBLICAL STORIES FOR MODERN COLLEGE LIFE

16

DAVID AND GOLIATH

___/___/_____

"The Lord," David added, "who rescued me from the power of both lions and bears, will rescue me from the power of this Philistine."

- 1 Samuel 17:37 (C.E.B.)

We all know the timeless story of David and Goliath. I remember sitting in your shoes, facing the daunting giants of academia, social pressures, and personal growth. David's story holds a remarkable lesson for all of us, whether we're fighting literal giants or figurative ones.

David, a young shepherd boy, stood before the towering warrior Goliath. On the surface, it seemed like an insurmountable battle. Goliath was armed to the teeth, a champion of war, while David had little more than a sling and stones. But what set David apart was his unwavering faith and courage.

In the face of impossible odds, David refused to be paralyzed by fear. He knew that God was his light and salvation, his stronghold. With this unshakable faith, he confronted the giant, aimed his sling, and let that stone fly. The rest is history—the giant fell, and David emerged victorious.

Just as David faced his giant with courage and trust in God's strength, you too can tackle the challenges of college life. Whether it's a tough exam, a daunting presentation, or personal struggles, remember that with faith, determination, and God as your stronghold, you can conquer the giants in your path.

Reflection: *Think about a current challenge or fear you're facing in college. How can you approach it with the courage and faith exhibited by David?*

Consider moments in your life when you've overcome seemingly impossible obstacles. What role did faith and determination play in your success?

Let us pray... Dear God, I thank you for the story of David and Goliath, a reminder of the courage and faith that can conquer our challenges. Help me face the giants in my college life with unwavering trust in Your strength. May I walk with the knowledge that You are my light and salvation. Amen.

17

GIDEON

___/___/_____

"When the angel of the Lord appeared to Gideon, he said, 'The Lord is with you, mighty warrior.'"

— JUDGES 6:12 (NIV)

Throughout life there are moments where we find ourselves face-to-face with self-doubt and insecurity, questioning our abilities and worthiness. I want to share with you the inspiring story of Gideon – a man who faced these very struggles and emerged victorious.

Gideon was a timid young man, living in a time of turmoil. He harbored self-doubt and insecurity, feeling unworthy of God's calling to lead his people to victory against a formidable enemy. Gideon's doubts were like heavy chains, holding him back from his true potential.

But something incredible happened. God saw Gideon's potential when Gideon couldn't see it himself. He reassured Gideon, saying, "I will be with you, and you will strike down all the Midianites together" (Judges 6:16, NIV), and an angel even referred to him as 'mighty warrior'. Thus, Gideon's journey to self-discovery and leadership had begun.

Gideon's story teaches us that even in moments of self-doubt and insecurity, God sees our potential and equips us with the strength to overcome our limitations. Just as Gideon found his courage and led a victorious battle, you too can conquer self-limiting beliefs and pursue your dreams.

You may not feel prepared, or like you have the skills right now, but you will gain them on your journey. Conquer self-doubt, pursue your dreams, and lead a victorious life just as Gideon did, with God as your guide and strength.

Reflection: *Reflect on a time when self-doubt or insecurity held you back from pursuing a goal. What steps can you take to overcome these self-limiting beliefs?*

Consider the people in your life who encourage and believe in you, much like God did for Gideon. How can you surround yourself with positive influences?

Let us pray... Dear God, I thank you for the story of Gideon, a reminder that you see our potential even when we doubt ourselves. Help me conquer self-doubt and insecurity as I pursue my dreams and fulfill my purpose. May I always remember that I can do all things through You who gives me strength. Amen.

18

TRUSTING GOD'S PROVISION - MATTHEW 6:25-34

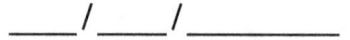

"But seek first his kingdom and his righteousness, and all these things will be given to you as well."

– MATTHEW 6:33 (NIV)

In our fast-paced and uncertain world, it's easy to be consumed by worries about the future—academics, career, relationships, and more. The words of Jesus, found in Matthew 6:25-34, offer us a profound lesson on trusting God's provision and embracing each day.

As the story goes Jesus spoke to a crowd, teaching them not to worry about their lives—what they would eat, drink, or wear. He reassured them that God cares for the birds of the air and the lilies of the field, and how much more does He care for us, His children. Worrying, Jesus taught, cannot add a single hour to our lives.

The heart of His message lies in seeking first God's kingdom and righteousness. By focusing on our faith journey and living in alignment with God's principles, we can trust that all our needs will be provided for.

Jesus encourages us to live one day at a time, knowing that God's grace is sufficient.

Instead of worrying about an uncertain future, you should prioritize living in the present moment. By trusting in His provision and focusing on the day at hand, you can find peace and fulfillment. God cares for you and your future is in His hands.

Reflection: *Reflect on the worries about the future that you carry. How can you shift your focus from anxiety to seeking God's kingdom in your daily life?*

Consider moments when you've seen God's provision and care in your journey. How can you build on those experiences to deepen your trust in Him?

Meditate on Matthew 6:33. How can you actively seek God's kingdom and righteousness in your college life, knowing that all things will be provided for?

Let us pray... Dear God, I thank you for the words of Jesus, reminding me not to worry about the future but to seek your kingdom and righteousness first. Help me let go of anxiety and trust in your provision. May I focus on each day with faith and gratitude. Amen.

19

MOSES

____ / ____ / _____

"Now go; I will help you speak and will teach you what to say."

- EXODUS 4:12 (NIV)

At many points in life you will find yourself at a crossroad, and may be hesitant to embrace your unique calling and take on leadership roles. The story of Moses, from Exodus 3-4, offers a powerful lesson in overcoming hesitations and growing into a strong leader.

Moses, a man with a stutter and self-doubts, was called by God to lead the Israelites out of Egypt. At first, he hesitated and questioned his abilities. But God assured him, saying, "Now go; I will help you speak and will teach you what to say."

Moses, despite his initial doubts, stepped into his calling and grew into one of the most renowned leaders in history. His journey teaches us that we, too, can overcome hesitations and become strong leaders in our own unique ways.

The lesson is clear—God equips those He calls. Like Moses, we may doubt ourselves and our capabilities, but with faith and God's guidance, we can embrace our callings and lead with confidence. Just as Moses grew into a strong leader, we too can overcome our doubts and become effective leaders in our academic pursuits, campus activities, and personal growth.

Reflection: *Reflect on any callings or leadership opportunities you've hesitated to embrace. What steps can you take to overcome your doubts and uncertainties?*

Consider moments in your life when you've felt God's guidance and empowerment. How can you draw upon those experiences as you step into leadership roles?

Meditate on Exodus 4:12. How can you trust in God's promise to help and teach you as you embrace your unique calling and leadership responsibilities?

Let us pray... Dear God, I thank you for the story of Moses, a reminder that you equip those you call. Help me overcome my hesitations and embrace my unique calling and leadership roles. May I have the faith to trust in your guidance and teaching. Amen.

20

THE SERENITY PRAYER

____ / ____ / _____

"And the peace of God, which transcends all understanding, will guard your hearts and your minds in Christ Jesus."

– Philippians 4:7 (NIV)

College life can be a whirlwind of challenges, decisions, and anxieties. The Serenity Prayer, rooted in Philippians 4:6-7, offers us a profound reminder to turn to God in prayer, trusting His peace to guard our hearts and minds. Serenity is a state of calm, peacefulness, and tranquility, free from stress or anxiety.

The Serenity Prayer

"God, grant me the serenity to accept the things I cannot change, courage to change the things I can, and wisdom to know the difference."

These words are a timeless guide for finding serenity amidst life's uncertainties.

In Philippians 4:6-7, we are urged not to be anxious but to bring our concerns to God in prayer. It promises that when we do, God's peace, which transcends all understanding, will guard our hearts and minds.

Prayer is a powerful tool for finding serenity, and God's peace surpasses all human understanding. By turning to Him in times of anxiety, we can experience a peace that goes beyond our circumstances.

Let's remember that in moments of stress and worry, we have the opportunity to find serenity through our faith, trusting that God's peace will guard our hearts and minds as we navigate the exciting yet demanding journey of college life.

Reflection: *Reflect on the anxieties you've faced in your college journey. How can you incorporate the Serenity Prayer's wisdom into your approach to life's challenges?*

Consider moments when prayer has brought you peace and clarity. How can you make prayer a consistent part of your college experience?

Let us pray... Dear God, I thank you for the Serenity Prayer, reminding me to bring my anxieties to you in prayer. Grant me the serenity, courage, and wisdom to find peace amidst life's challenges. May your transcendent peace guard my heart and mind as I journey through college. Amen.

21

JONAH AND THE WHALE

____ / ____ / _____

"In my distress, I called to the Lord, and he answered me. From deep in the realm of the dead I called for help, and you listened to my cry."

– JONAH 2:2 (NIV)

Jonah's journey in the Book of Jonah is a tale of running from God's call, facing consequences, and ultimately learning about obedience and second chances—themes that often resonate with the struggles of finding one's path in college.

Jonah was called by God to go to Nineveh and deliver a message, but he fled in the opposite direction. He found himself in the belly of a great fish, a consequence of his disobedience. In the depths of his despair, Jonah called out to God, and God rescued him. Jonah emerged from the fish with a newfound understanding of obedience.

Jonah's story reminds us that, like him, we may sometimes run from our callings or make choices that lead to challenges. Yet, God is a God of second chances. When we call out in distress, He listens and guides us back onto the path He has set for us.

God offers us second chances, even when we've strayed from His call. Just as Jonah learned about obedience and redemption, we can find our way back to our purpose and calling, no matter how lost we may feel. Use this story to trust in God's guidance as you traverse the challenges of finding your own path in college.

Reflection: *Reflect on moments when you've felt uncertain about your path in college. How can Jonah's journey inspire you to embrace obedience and seek your calling?*

Consider times when you've faced consequences for your choices. How can you turn those experiences into opportunities for growth and redemption?

Meditate on Jonah 2:2. How can you trust in God's willingness to answer your cry for help and guide you toward your purpose in college?

Let us pray... Dear God, I thank you for Jonah's story, a reminder that you offer second chances and guidance, even when I've strayed from your path. Help me embrace obedience and find my calling in college, knowing that you listen to my cries for help. May I trust in your redemption. Amen.

Bible Study - The Story of Paul

2 Corinthians 11:24-28

The story of Paul's perseverance, as recorded in 2 Corinthians 11:24-28, serves as a remarkable testament to enduring faith in the face of adversity. As college men navigating the complexities of modern academic and personal challenges, we can draw inspiration from Paul's unwavering commitment to his faith and mission. This Bible study will explore Paul's experiences, encouraging us to persevere through our own trials, maintain our faith, and find strength in Christ.

Reading: First, read the passage from 2 Corinthians 11:24-28 to understand Paul's account of his trials and hardships.

Discussion:

1. **Trials and Endurance**: Reflect on the trials and hardships Paul endured in his mission to spread the Gospel. What are some of the challenges you face as a college student, and how can Paul's endurance inspire you to persevere?

2. **Maintaining Faith**: Despite the difficulties he faced, Paul remained steadfast in his faith. How can Paul's example help you maintain and strengthen your faith during your college journey?

3. **The Cost of Discipleship**: Paul's account highlights the sacrifices he made for his faith. What sacrifices might you need to make to live out your faith while pursuing your dreams and aspirations in college?

4. **Facing Opposition**: Paul encountered opposition and persecution. How do you respond to opposition or challenges related to your faith or values, and what can you learn from Paul's response?

5. **Strength in Weakness**: Paul emphasizes finding strength in Christ's grace during times of weakness. How can relying on God's grace help you navigate your weaknesses and challenges in college?

6. **Perseverance and Purpose**: Reflect on the connection between perseverance and purpose in Paul's life. How can maintaining perseverance align with your purpose or calling as a college student?

7. **Support and Community**: Paul had a network of supporters who encouraged and prayed for him. How important is a supportive community in your college life, and how can you build or strengthen such relationships?

Reflection: *Consider your current challenges and hardships in college. How can you apply the lessons of Paul's perseverance to overcome these obstacles while maintaining your faith and purpose?*

Let us pray... Dear God, as we reflect on the inspiring journey of Paul, who persevered through trials and hardships for the sake of his faith and mission, we seek Your guidance and strength. Grant us the perseverance to face the challenges of college life, the wisdom to maintain our faith, and the resolve to align our purposes with Your will. In moments of weakness, may we find strength in Your grace. Amen.

Optional: Read more about Paul's life and writings in the New Testament, particularly in the Book of Acts and his epistles. Reflect on how his experiences can further inspire and guide you in your college journey.

NAVIGATING NIGHTLIFE

23

FUN AND RESPONSIBILITY

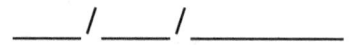

"There is a time for everything, and a season for every activity under the heavens."

– Ecclesiastes 3:1 (NIV)

Nightlife is a huge part of the excitement of college. It's not wrong to love partying- but we need to learn to enjoy it while keeping our values intact. It's all about finding the sweet spot between fun and responsibility.

While these experiences buzz with energy and opportunities to make unforgettable memories, it also presents choices that can impact our integrity and values. It's easy to get caught up in the thrill of the moment, especially when alcohol is involved. It could be choices related to excessive drinking, peer pressure, or engaging in behaviors that go against our moral compass. These choices might seem enticing in the heat of the night, but they can cast shadows on our sense of self and leave us with regrets.

God calls us to find joy in life, to celebrate with friends, and to make the most of our college years. Yet, He also encourages us to maintain our integrity and values in all we do. It's about striking a balance between enjoying the moment and making responsible choices. It's about savoring the season of college life responsibly.

Reflection: *Reflect on past experiences. Were there moments when you felt the balance between fun and responsibility was challenging? How can you approach such situations differently in the future?*

Consider the values and principles that guide your life. How can you ensure that your choices during nightlife align with these values?

Meditate on Ecclesiastes 3:1. How can you embrace the joy of college nightlife while also being responsible in your actions?

Let us pray... Dear God, I thank you for the exciting season of college life and the opportunities to enjoy nightlife with friends. Help me strike a balance between fun and responsibility, making choices that align with my values. May I find joy in each moment while honoring you. Amen.

24

PEER PRESSURE AND STANDING FIRM

____ / ____ / _____

"But Daniel resolved not to defile himself with the royal food and wine, and he asked the chief official for permission not to defile himself this way."

– DANIEL 1:8 (NIV)

Let's dive into a topic that's all too familiar: peer pressure. It's those moments when the crowd's pull seems irresistible, and it can challenge our convictions. But we have biblical wisdom and role models like Daniel to guide us.

Daniel, a young man, faced a situation where he was pressured to conform to the ways of the Babylonian royal court. He was offered the king's rich food and wine, but he resolved not to defile himself in this way. Despite the social pressures and temptations around him, he stood firm in his faith and convictions.

Peer pressure in college nightlife can be equally intense, whether it's about excessive drinking, compromising values, or going against our beliefs. But, like Daniel, we can resolve not to defile ourselves and stay true to our convictions.

The lesson here is about standing firm in the face of peer pressure. Just as Daniel held onto his faith and values, we can draw inspiration from his resolve to maintain our convictions even in the midst of social temptations. Peer pressure may surround us, but with faith and determination, we can stay true to our beliefs and make choices that honor our values.

Reflection: *Reflect on instances when you've felt pressured to go along with the crowd during nightlife. How did you respond, and how might you approach such situations differently in the future?*

Consider your convictions and beliefs. How can you strengthen your resolve to maintain them in the midst of peer pressure?

Meditate on Daniel 1:8. How can you draw inspiration from Daniel's example and stand firm in your convictions during college nightlife?

Let us pray... Dear God, I thank you for the example of Daniel, who stood firm in his convictions even when faced with peer pressure. Help me draw strength from his resolve to maintain my faith and values during college nightlife. Grant me the courage to resist the pressures around me and stand firm in what I believe. Amen.

25

Choosing Your Company Wisely

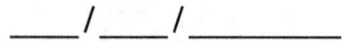

"Walk with the wise and become wise, for a companion of fools suffers harm."

— Proverbs 13:20 (NIV)

In the vibrant tapestry of life, one significant thread is the company we keep. It's about surrounding ourselves with positive influences, just as the Prodigal Son's story teaches us.

The Prodigal Son, known for his reckless living, had companions who influenced his choices. Their company led him down a path of extravagance and indulgence, eventually leading to his downfall. It wasn't until he realized the impact of his choices and changed his company that his life began to transform.

In college nightlife, the people we surround ourselves with can greatly influence our decisions. Positive influences can inspire us to make wise choices, while negative companions may lead us down paths we'd later regret. It's a reminder that, as Proverbs 13:20 suggests, walking with the wise helps us become wise, while being a companion of fools can lead to harm.

Choose your company wisely.

Just as the Prodigal Son learned the significance of positive influences, we too can thrive when we surround ourselves with friends who uplift, support, and inspire us to make responsible choices.

Reflection: *Reflect on the impact of the company you've kept during college nightlife. How have your friends influenced your decisions?*

Consider the qualities of positive influences. How can you seek out and nurture friendships that inspire wise choices?

Let us pray... Dear God, I thank you for the valuable lesson from the Prodigal Son's story, reminding me of the importance of choosing my company wisely. Help me discern positive influences and seek friendships that inspire responsible choices during college nightlife. May I be a source of wisdom and encouragement to others as well. Amen.

26

SETTING BOUNDARIES AND LIMITS

___/___/_____

"Above all else, guard your heart, for everything you do flows from it."

– PROVERBS 4:23 (NIV)

A topic that holds immense significance in college life and nightlife is Setting Boundaries and Limits. It's about finding the strength within ourselves to resist temptation, just as Joseph did.

Joseph, a man of great integrity, found himself in a challenging situation. Potiphar's wife relentlessly pursued him, trying to seduce him into an immoral relationship. But Joseph understood the importance of boundaries and limits. He firmly refused her advances, saying, "How then could I do such a wicked thing and sin against God?" (Genesis 39:9, NIV).

In college, especially when we're partying, we encounter situations where boundaries can be tested. It might involve peer pressure, temptation, or compromising situations. However, Joseph's story teaches us that establishing boundaries is not a sign of weakness but a testament to our strength and commitment to honor God and our values.

Just as Joseph resisted temptation, we too can find the inner strength to protect our hearts and stay true to our principles during college nightlife.

Reflection: *Reflect on moments when you've felt tempted to cross your boundaries during college nightlife. How did you respond, and what were the outcomes?*

Consider the boundaries you've set for yourself. How can you strengthen and communicate them to ensure they're respected?

Let us pray... Dear God, I thank you for the story of Joseph, a reminder of the strength that comes from setting boundaries and limits. Help me guard my heart and preserve my integrity during college nightlife. Grant me the courage to say no to temptation, knowing that it honors you and my values. Amen.

27

THE MORNING AFTER

"Search me, God, and know my heart; test me and know my anxious thoughts. See if there is any offensive way in me, and lead me in the way everlasting."

– PSALM 139:23-24 (NIV)

We've ventured into the realm of college nightlife, but now it's time to ponder what happens next – the morning after.

Just as Psalm 139:23-24 implores us to search our hearts and minds, we, too, can examine our actions, thoughts, and choices. In these moments of reflection, we can learn from our mistakes, acknowledge our growth, and make positive changes. It's about using every experience, even the missteps, as opportunities for personal growth and learning.

Nights of overindulgence, peer pressure, conflicts, time management challenges, and positive encounters. These experiences, both challenging and joyful, provide us with opportunities for growth and learning. As we search our hearts and minds in the quiet hours of the morning after, we can recognize areas where we need improvement and celebrate personal growth milestones. From the discomfort of overindulgence to the importance of standing firm in our values, every experience becomes a lesson. Through reflection, we gain wisdom, ensuring that each night out contributes not only to our college memories but also to our personal development.

By searching our hearts and minds, we can identify areas where we may need improvement and find the path to lasting, positive change.

Reflection: *Think about the recent nightlife experiences you've had in college. Are there moments you wish you had handled differently? How can you learn from those experiences?*

Consider the personal growth you've undergone during your college journey. What positive changes have you made, and how can you continue to grow?

Let us pray... Dear God, I thank you for the gift of reflection and growth, especially in the context of college nightlife. As I search my heart and mind, help me identify areas where I can learn and grow from my experiences. Guide me in making positive changes and walking in the way everlasting. Amen.

Bible Study - The Parable of the Prodigal Son

Luke 15:11-32

The Parable of the Prodigal Son is a powerful story of redemption and the boundless love of God. It speaks to our human experiences of making mistakes, feeling lost, and seeking forgiveness. As college men navigating the world of nightlife, we encounter various situations, some positive and others potentially harmful. This parable can offer valuable insights into making wise choices and understanding God's grace amid the nightlife adventures.

Reading: First, read Luke 15:11-32 (The Parable of the Prodigal Son).

Discussion:

1. **Prodigal Living**: In the parable, the younger son makes choices that lead him into a life of recklessness and excess during his time away. Have you ever felt the temptation to live a "prodigal" lifestyle during your college nightlife experiences? What were the consequences?

2. **Turning Point**: What eventually causes the younger son to reconsider his choices and return home? Have you experienced a turning point in your own life or in the life of someone you know that led to positive change after a period of mistakes or missteps?

3. **Unconditional Love**: The father in the parable represents God's unconditional love and forgiveness. How does this portrayal of the father's love impact your understanding of God's love, especially in the context of nightlife-related mistakes?

4. **Resentment and Forgiveness**: The elder son initially reacts with resentment when his younger brother returns home. How can feelings of resentment or judgment affect our relationships with others in college, especially when they make mistakes or have different nightlife experiences?

5. **Redemption and Restoration**: What does the story teach us about redemption and the possibility of restoring relationships after making mistakes or poor choices? How can this apply to college life and the challenges of nightlife?

6. **Wisdom and Choices**: Reflect on the lessons the younger son

learned during his time away. How can these lessons inform our choices during college, especially in the context of nightlife? What wisdom can we draw from his experiences?

Reflection: *Think about a specific situation in your college nightlife experiences when you made a mistake or faced uncertainty. How can the Parable of the Prodigal Son inspire you to seek redemption, show forgiveness, or make wiser choices moving forward?*

Let us pray... Dear God, we thank You for the profound lessons Your Word imparts to us. May the story of the Prodigal Son remind us of Your boundless love, forgiveness, and the potential for redemption in our own lives. As we navigate the complexities of college and nightlife, grant us the wisdom to make choices that honor You and reflect Your grace. Amen.

SELF-CARE

29

CARING FOR THE TEMPLE

___ / ___ / _____

"Do you not know that your bodies are temples of the Holy Spirit, who is in you, whom you have received from God? You are not your own."

- 1 CORINTHIANS 6:19 (NIV)

We've all been there - the late-night study sessions, the quick-to-grab junk food, and the mountains of stress that college can bring. Caring for the temple that is your body is crucial to maintain peak mental and physical health.

Picture this: It's exam week, and you're burning the midnight oil. You've got energy drinks and snacks littered across your desk. You've pushed through fatigue and hunger to keep studying. But here's the twist - this time, I want you to hit pause.

I know that acing exams is essential, but so is taking care of the temple God has given you - your body. That energy drink may provide a short burst, but it's no substitute for a good night's sleep. Those snacks? Well, they might keep you full, but they won't fuel your body properly.

You see, our bodies are temples of the Holy Spirit. They're a divine gift, and we're entrusted with their care. Neglecting your physical and mental well-being not only affects your health and college experience but also your connection with God.

Self-care isn't selfish; it's an act of stewardship. Just as you care for your faith, relationships, and academics, remember to care for your physical and mental health. This might mean scheduling regular exercise, eating balanced meals, or taking short breaks to clear your mind. By honoring your body, you're honoring God.

Reflection: *How do you currently prioritize your physical and mental well-being amidst the demands of college life?*

Consider the ways in which you might be neglecting self-care. What small changes can you make to improve your temple's care?

How can self-care impact your relationship with God and your ability to fulfill your purpose in college?

Let us pray... Dear God, in the midst of my college journey, help me remember that my body is Your temple. Grant me the wisdom to prioritize self-care, honoring the gift You've given me. May my physical and mental well-being reflect my reverence for You. Amen.

30

SABBATH REST AND SLEEP HYGIENE

___/___/_____

"Come to me, all you who are weary and burdened, and I will give you rest."

- MATTHEW 11:28 (NIV)

Ah at last, the weekend is here and everyone seems to be making plans! You've got assignments to catch up on, social events to attend, and a to-do list that never ends. Sound familiar? It did to me too.

Now, let's take a step back and reflect on the biblical concept of Sabbath. God Himself rested on the seventh day after creating the world. It's a divine reminder that rest is as vital as work. In the midst of our bustling lives, taking time to rest isn't just a luxury; it's a necessity.

Alongside Sabbath rest, consider the importance of quality sleep. Those late-night study sessions may seem productive, but sleep is when your body and mind rejuvenate. It impacts your memory, mood, and overall well-being.

Create a restful sleep environment

Your sleep environment plays a vital role in ensuring restful sleep. Make your bed a sanctuary of comfort and peace. Invest in a good mattress and pillows that provide support. Keep your room dark with blackout curtains, maintain a comfortable temperature, and minimize noise disturbances. Remove or cover electronic devices with LED lights, and choose soft, breathable bedding materials.

Improve your sleep hygiene!

Good sleep hygiene is essential for restorative sleep. Establish a consistent sleep schedule by going to bed and waking up at the same time daily. Limit daytime naps and avoid caffeine and alcohol close to bedtime. Engage in regular physical activity but finish intense workouts a few hours before sleep. Develop a calming bedtime routine to signal to your body that it's time to wind down. To help you can set a 'wind-down' alarm to remind you to start your bedtime routine consistently. Finally, reserve your bed for sleep and intimate activities only. Avoid working or studying in bed.

Remember, God invites us to find rest in Him. By embracing the concept of Sabbath and maintaining good sleep hygiene, you're not neglecting your responsibilities but acknowledging that true productivity comes from a rested soul.

Reflection: *How do you currently approach rest in your college routine? Is there room for improvement?*

Are there times when you've neglected rest and paid the price for it? Reflect on those experiences.

What changes can you make to prioritize Sabbath rest and better sleep hygiene in your life?

Let us pray... Dear God, in the midst of my college journey, help me honor the concept of Sabbath as You intended. Grant me the discipline to establish good sleep hygiene practices. May I find rest and renewal in Your presence, trusting that it will enrich my overall well-being. Amen.

31

CREATIVE EXPLORATION

___ / ___ / _____

"In the beginning, God created the heavens and the earth."

- GENESIS 1:1

Your college journey can sometimes feel like an endless to-do list, and self-care might take a back seat. However, there's a beautiful form of self-care that you can weave into your life.

Engaging in creative activities can serve as a powerful retreat for your mind and spirit. Just as God created the world, we have the ability to create, whether through art, music, writing, or other forms of expression. These activities provide an opportunity to step away from the demands of college life and find moments of renewal. Embrace your creativity as a gift from God, allowing it to rejuvenate your energy and bring mental clarity.

"For we are God's masterpiece. He has created us anew in Christ Jesus, so we can do the good things he planned for us long ago."

- EPHESIANS 2:10

Imagine a canvas waiting to be painted, a blank page ready for words, or an empty room echoing with music. These are spaces where you can explore and express your creativity, and in doing so, experience renewal. Just as God created you as His masterpiece, you have the power to create. Artistic exploration allows you to recharge, find vitality, and connect with the divine source of creativity.

Just as God is the ultimate creator, He has blessed you with the ability to create in various forms. When you engage in artistic activities, you tap into a wellspring of renewal and vitality.

Here are some creative avenues you can explore:

1. **Painting or Drawing:** Whether you're a seasoned artist or picking up a brush for the first time, painting or drawing can be incredibly therapeutic. Don't worry about creating a masterpiece; focus on the process and the joy of self-expression.

2. **Writing:** Journaling, poetry, short stories, or even song lyrics can be a channel for your thoughts and emotions. It's a way to reflect on your experiences and gain clarity.

3. **Music:** Playing an instrument, creating music, or simply listening mindfully to your favorite tunes can be a form of artistic rejuvenation. Music has the power to uplift and inspire.

4. **Photography:** Capturing moments through a lens allows you to see the world from a different perspective. It encourages you to notice beauty in the ordinary.

5. **Crafts and DIY Projects:** Building, sculpting, or crafting can be both fun and meditative. You might surprise yourself with

your creative ingenuity.

6. **Dance:** Whether you're a trained dancer or just love to move, dancing is a fantastic way to let loose, release stress, and feel more alive.

7. **Cooking and Baking:** Preparing a meal with creativity and intention can be an art form in itself. Try new recipes, experiment with flavors, and savor the results.

Remember, the goal isn't perfection but the process. In these moments of artistic exploration, you can find renewal and connect with the purpose God has for you. Just as He created you, you can create, and in doing so, you honor the body as a temple of the Holy Spirit.

Reflection: *Which creative activity resonates with you the most, and why?*

When was the last time you engaged in artistic exploration, and how did it make you feel?

Can you think of a creative project you'd like to explore, start, or complete?

What barriers might be preventing you from incorporating more creative moments into your routine? How can you overcome them?

Let us pray... Dear God, thank you for blessing me with the gift of creativity. Help me embrace artistic exploration as a means of self-care and renewal. May my creative endeavors bring me closer to You and help me better understand the good things You have planned for me. In Your name, I pray. Amen.

32

EVENING EXERCISE

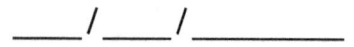

"In peace, I will lie down and sleep, for you alone, Lord, make me dwell in safety."

– PSALM 4:8 (NIV)

The day's chaos has subsided, and the night is quiet. Instead of diving into another Netflix binge or scrolling through social media, why not choose a different path? Let's roll out your yoga mat or find a comfortable spot for some gentle stretching exercises.

Why choose yoga and stretching for your evening routine? It's simple. These practices provide a profound way to release the accumulated stress and tension from the day. Yoga, in particular, blends physical postures with mindful breathing, creating a soothing rhythm that calms both body and mind. Stretching, on the other hand, lengthens tight muscles, improving flexibility and easing physical discomfort.

Psalm 4:8 speaks of finding peace before sleep, knowing that God is our refuge. Yoga and stretching can help you achieve this peace. They prepare your body for rest, promoting better sleep quality and a sense of serenity.

Benefits:

1. **Stress Reduction:** Yoga and stretching help lower cortisol levels, the stress hormone, promoting relaxation and reducing anxiety.

2. **Improved Sleep:** The calming effect of these practices can lead to deeper, more restful sleep, helping you wake up refreshed.

3. **Physical Well-being:** Stretching enhances flexibility, reduces muscle tension, and improves posture, preventing discomfort or pain.

4. **Mental Clarity:** Yoga encourages mindfulness, allowing you to let go of worries and focus on the present moment.

Let's remember that in the stillness of the night, we can find God's peace through simple practices like yoga and stretching. These moments of self-care are not just about our physical health but also about nurturing our spiritual connection and preparing ourselves for a new day in college life.

Reflection: *Reflect on your bedtime routine. Do you set aside time for evening exercise or self-care? If not, how might incorporating it benefit your overall well-being?*

Are there opportunities to incorporate yoga and stretching to unwind and prepare for sleep?

Consider the difference in your sleep quality when you practice yoga and stretching versus when you don't. How does it affect your daily life and your connection with God?

Let us pray... Dear God, as I prepare for rest, I seek your peace and safety. Thank you for the gift of evening yoga and stretching, which allows me to release the day's burdens and find tranquility. May these practices not only benefit my physical well-being but also draw me closer to you. In this peaceful state, grant me restful sleep and renewed strength for the days ahead. Amen.

33

OVERCOMING REGRET

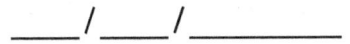

"Cast your cares on the Lord and he will sustain you; he will never let the righteous be shaken."

– PSALM 55:22 (NIV)

Do you have any nagging worries, regrets, or anxieties that you can't seem to shake? The act of surrender and acceptance can help us to restore our joy and peace by leaving our past behind us.

It's easy for worries or regrets to stack up. Especially in college where we have countless new opportunities pop up so often. Regrets, like heavy baggage, can slow us down and prevent us from reaching our full potential. They are the echoes of past mistakes, reminding us of what went wrong. Each mistake we make can serve as a valuable lesson if we allow it to. Instead of being a source of shame or frustration, our missteps can become catalysts for growth and transformation. However, dwelling on regrets hinders our ability to move forward with purpose, and peace. The wisdom of Psalm 55:22 reminds us that we have a loving God to whom we can cast our cares.

Letting go is not a sign of weakness but an act of trust in God's sustaining power. Imagine the freedom of unburdening your heart, releasing the anxieties and regrets that keep you awake at night. As you do so, you open the door to greater joy and peace in your life.

Prayer for letting go:

Before you lay down to rest, take a moment to pray. Confide in God like a trusted friend, sharing your worries, regrets, and anxieties. As you pour out your heart, visualize these burdens leaving you, floating away like leaves on a gentle stream. Place them in God's capable hands, knowing that He will sustain you and bring you peace. Let this prayer be your nightly practice, releasing what holds you back and allowing you to embrace the serenity God offers.

Reflection: *What worries or regrets have you been carrying with you lately? How might letting go of them positively impact your life?*

How can you incorporate the practice of surrendering your concerns to God into your daily routine?

Reflect on moments when you have experienced joy and peace after letting go of a burden. How can these experiences inspire your faith?

Let us pray... Dear God, tonight, I choose to let go of my worries, regrets, and anxieties. I trust that You will sustain me and fill me with Your peace. Thank You for the promise of serenity that comes through surrender. Amen.

34

INNER PEACE

___ / ___ / _____

"You will keep in perfect peace those whose minds are steadfast because they trust in you."

- ISAIAH 26:3

During the college chaos, wouldn't it be wonderful to discover a timeless secret to inner peace and tranquility? Well, you're in luck. Ancient practices like mindfulness and meditation hold the key.

Imagine this: You're racing against the clock, trying to finish a paper, or studying for an important exam. Your mind is a hurricane of thoughts, worry, and stress. It's in moments like these that practicing mindfulness and meditation can make all the difference.

Mindfulness is simply being present in the moment, acknowledging your thoughts and feelings without judgment. It's about finding tranquility amid the chaos. Meditation, on the other hand, is a focused mental exercise that calms your mind and helps you gain clarity.

One practical way to incorporate these practices into your life is by engaging in relaxation techniques before sleep. Deep breathing exercises, for instance, can signal to your body that it's time to unwind. As you lie in bed, take slow, deep breaths, in through your nose and out through your mouth. Let go of any tension with each exhale. Feel your body and mind becoming more relaxed.

Why is this important? Because a peaceful mind leads to better rest and rejuvenation. When you sleep well, you wake up refreshed, ready to tackle the challenges of the day.

But let's take it one step further. Seek God's presence in these moments of mindfulness and meditation. Just as He stilled the stormy seas, He can calm the storms within you. In His presence, you find a deeper sense of calm that surpasses all understanding.

Reflection: *How do you typically react when you're stressed or overwhelmed with college work?*

Have you ever tried mindfulness or meditation before? If so, what was your experience?

How do you envision incorporating God's presence into your moments of mindfulness and meditation?

Let us pray... Dear God, in the midst of life's chaos, I seek Your peace. Help me cultivate inner tranquility through mindfulness and meditation. As I practice relaxation techniques, may I find restful sleep and wake with a rejuvenated spirit. Be with me in these moments, Lord, and grant me Your perfect peace. Amen.

Bible Study - Mary and Martha

___ / ___ / _____

Luke 10:38-42

The story of Mary and Martha in Luke 10:38-42 offers valuable insights into the importance of balancing our daily activities with moments of rest, reflection, and self-care. Just as Mary chose to sit at Jesus' feet and listen, we can learn from her example how to prioritize our spiritual well-being and find inner peace amidst the busyness of life. This Bible study will delve into the story of Mary and Martha, exploring various aspects of self-care and how we can incorporate them into our college lives.

Reading: First, read the passage from Luke 10:38-42 to understand the story of Mary and Martha's encounter with Jesus.

Discussion:

1. **Prioritizing Spiritual Nourishment**: Mary chose to sit and learn from Jesus. How can we prioritize spiritual nourishment and reflection in our daily lives?

2. **Balancing Activity and Rest**: Martha was busy with many tasks, but Jesus commended Mary for choosing rest. How can we find a healthy balance between our college activities and moments of rest and self-care?

3. **Overcoming Regret**: Martha initially felt regret about her choice of busyness. How can we learn from our regrets and make positive changes in our self-care routines?

4. **Inner Peace**: Mary found inner peace by sitting at Jesus' feet. What practices or habits can help us nurture inner peace and emotional well-being?

5. **Sabbath Rest**: How can the concept of Sabbath rest, setting aside time for reflection and worship, benefit our college experience?

6. **Caring for the Temple**: Our bodies are temples of the Holy Spirit. What steps can we take to care for our physical and mental health as an act of worship?

Reflection: *Reflect on the story of Mary and Martha and how it relates to various aspects of self-care. Consider how you can incorporate these practices into your college life to find balance, inner peace, and spiritual nourishment.*

Let us pray... Dear God, we are reminded of Mary and Martha's encounter with Jesus, where we learn the importance of balancing activity and rest, nurturing our spiritual well-being, and caring for our bodies as temples of the Holy Spirit. As we strive to find equilibrium in our college lives, grant us the wisdom to prioritize self-care and seek moments of inner peace and reflection. May our actions and choices align with Your guidance. Amen.

CONNECTING WITH GOD

36

PRAYERFUL REFLECTION

"May these words of my mouth and this meditation of my heart be pleasing in your sight, Lord, my Rock and my Redeemer."

– PSALM 19:14 (NIV)

I'd like to share a secret with you - the source of my strength throughout my college journey. It's the practice of prayerful reflection at the close of each day. As the world around you grows quieter and you find a serene moment in the stillness of your room, you have the opportunity to open your heart and mind to God. Here you can share the experiences, challenges, and blessings that have colored your day. It's not just a conversation; it's a sacred exchange - a heart-to-heart with your Creator and Friend.

Why engage in prayerful reflection at the end of the day? It's a powerful practice that helps you find solace and connection with the Divine. In those moments of openness and vulnerability, you lay bare your thoughts and feelings before God, seeking His guidance and offering gratitude for the blessings you've encountered.

Psalm 19:14 reminds us that our words and meditations should be pleasing to the Lord. Prayerful reflection allows you to align your heart and mind with God's will, fostering a deeper connection with your Creator and Redeemer.

Let's remember that in the quiet moments of prayerful reflection, we draw closer to God and find solace in His presence. This practice not only enriches our spiritual lives but also provides a source of guidance and inner peace in the midst of college life's challenges and joys.

Reflection: *Reflect on your current evening routine. How can you incorporate prayerful reflection into it to nurture your spiritual connection?*

Consider the impact of sharing both your joys and struggles with God in your daily reflections. How might it deepen your faith and resilience?

Let us pray... Dear God, as I come before you in prayerful reflection, I seek your presence and guidance. May the words of my heart and the thoughts of my mind be pleasing in your sight, my Rock and Redeemer. Thank you for the opportunity to share my experiences, challenges, and blessings with you. In this sacred connection, I find peace and strength for the journey ahead. Amen.

37

CREATING A SACRED SPACE

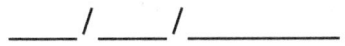

"Do not come any closer," God said. "Take off your sandals, for the place where you are standing is holy ground."

— EXODUS 3:5 (NIV)

Have you ever considered creating a sacred space for prayer in your dorm or room? A place that's exclusively yours where you can retreat to find stillness and communion with God. It's more than just a physical setting; it's a sacred sanctuary.

Let's delve into the importance of creating a sacred space. Think of it as a tangible invitation to connect with the Divine, a physical reminder that your spiritual journey matters amidst the hustle and bustle of college life. This space can be as simple or elaborate as you like, but its essence lies in its ability to foster a sense of peace and reverence.

Consider placing a soft rug, a comfortable chair, or a cushion in your chosen spot. Add elements that resonate with you, like a candle, a small plant, or a cherished book of prayers. These objects serve as conduits, helping you transition from the external world to your inner sanctuary.

In the Bible, we find the concept of sacred space when God spoke to

Moses from the burning bush. God's presence made that ordinary place holy ground. Similarly, your sacred space can become a hallowed spot where you encounter the Divine in the midst of your college journey.

Let's remember that our sacred space is not just a physical location; it's a sacred portal to a deeper connection with God. It's an intentional act of nurturing your spiritual well-being, and an invitation to encounter the Divine and to find a haven of peace and connection within your room.

Reflection: *Reflect on your current living situation in college. Do you have a space dedicated to prayer and reflection? If not, consider how you could create one.*

Consider the objects and elements that would make your sacred space meaningful. What resonates with you, and how can these items enhance your spiritual connection?

Meditate on Exodus 3:5. How does the idea of the ground being holy when God is present inspire you to create a sacred space for your own spiritual encounters?

Let us pray... Dear God, as I embark on this journey of creating a sacred space in my college room, I seek your presence and guidance. May this space become a sanctuary where I can connect with you, find solace, and nurture my spirit. Amen.

38

LISTENING IN SILENCE

"He says, 'Be still, and know that I am God; I will be exalted among the nations, I will be exalted in the earth.'"

— PSALM 46:10 (NIV)

Shh, can you hear that?

Silence often speaks louder than words. In our noisy world, where notifications, conversations, and distractions are constant companions, embracing silence can be a profound act of spiritual discipline. It's in those quiet moments that we can truly listen to the gentle whisper of God's voice.

Consider incorporating silence into your daily routine, whether it's in the morning, between classes, or as you wind down in the evening. Find a comfortable spot, sit in stillness, and simply breathe. Let your thoughts settle, and as you do, you create a sacred space for God to speak to your heart.

Psalm 46:10 reminds us to "be still, and know that I am God." In the hushed moments of silence, we come to know and experience God's presence in a way that transcends words. It's a place of communion where God's voice becomes clearer, guiding us through the challenges and joys of college life.

In the quiet of silence, we find the space to encounter God's voice and presence, offering us clarity and reassurance as we navigate the challenges and joys of life.

Reflection: *Reflect on your current daily routine. Are there moments of silence or stillness? How could you intentionally incorporate quiet moments into your day?*

Consider the impact of silence on your spiritual life. How might listening in silence help you navigate the challenges and joys of college with greater clarity and peace?

Meditate on Psalm 46:10. What does it mean to you to "be still" and know that God is present, especially in the context of college life?

Let us pray... Dear God, as I embrace the practice of listening in silence, I seek your presence and guidance. May the moments of stillness become a sanctuary where I hear your voice, find clarity, and connect with you. Amen.

THE EXAMEN PRAYER

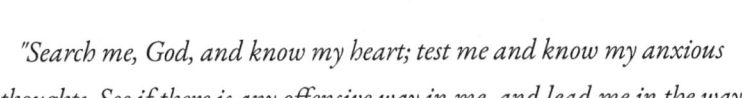

"Search me, God, and know my heart; test me and know my anxious thoughts. See if there is any offensive way in me, and lead me in the way everlasting."

– PSALM 139:23-24 (NIV)

The Examen prayer is a beautiful and ancient practice that offers us an opportunity to intentionally engage with God. It involves several steps, but at its core, it's about reflection, gratitude, and seeking God's guidance.

1. **Preparation:** Find a quiet and comfortable space. Invite God into your presence, acknowledging His presence with you.

2. **Review:** Begin by reviewing your day. Look back on your experiences, conversations, and emotions. Notice the moments that stand out, both positive and challenging.

3. **Gratitude:** Express gratitude to God for the blessings and joys you've experienced throughout the day. Be thankful for the people, opportunities, and moments that have brought you joy.

4. **Awareness:** Ask God for insight and awareness. Where did you feel His presence today? Where did you perhaps miss an opportunity to connect with Him?

5. **Confession:** Reflect on any moments where you fell short, made mistakes, or missed the mark. Seek God's forgiveness and guidance for the future.

6. **Resolution:** Finally, make a resolution for the future. How can you carry the lessons and insights from this reflection into the days ahead? What changes or growth do you aspire to?

Psalm 139:23-24 encourages us to invite God to search our hearts and lead us in the way everlasting. The Examen prayer is a practical way to engage in deep self-reflection. It is a transformative practice that invites us to walk hand in hand with God, reflecting on our daily journey. It helps us to recognize His presence, find gratitude in the ordinary, and seek His guidance in the days ahead.

Reflection: *Reflect on your current daily routine. Are there moments of intentional reflection and connection with God? How could you incorporate the Examen prayer into your daily life?*

Meditate on Psalm 139:23-24. What does it mean to invite God to search your heart and lead you in the way everlasting, especially within the context of college life?

Let us pray... Dear God, as I embrace the Examen prayer, I open my heart to your presence and guidance. May this practice become a sacred space where I reflect on my day, find gratitude, and seek your wisdom. Just as the psalmist prayed, "Search me, God, and know my heart," I invite you to search my heart and lead me in the way everlasting. Amen.

Bible Study - Elijah on Mount Horeb

1 Kings 19:9-18

The story of Elijah on Mount Horeb in 1 Kings 19:9-18 provides us with profound insights into how we can deepen our connection with God through prayer, reflection, and seeking His presence in our lives. Just as Elijah encountered God in a quiet whisper, we can learn valuable lessons about the ways in which we can connect with God amidst the busyness of our college lives. This study will delve into the story of Elijah and explore practical ways to strengthen our connection with God.

Reading: First, read the passage from 1 Kings 19:9-18 to understand Elijah's encounter with God on Mount Horeb.

Discussion Questions:

1. **Finding God in the Silence**: Elijah encountered God in a gentle whisper. In what ways can we create moments of silence and stillness in our daily lives to connect with God?

2. **Listening to God's Voice**: Elijah listened to God's voice and received guidance. How can we cultivate an attentive heart and discern God's voice in our own lives?

3. **Seeking Solitude**: Elijah withdrew to a solitary place on the mountain. How can finding moments of solitude or creating a sacred space enhance our connection with God?

4. **Dealing with Desolation**: Elijah initially felt desolation and despair. How can we learn from his experience and seek God's presence during difficult times in college?

5. **Rekindling Faith**: Elijah's encounter with God reignited his faith and purpose. How can connecting with God similarly rekindle our faith and help us find direction and purpose in our college journey?

6. **Reflecting on God's Presence**: After his encounter, Elijah reflected on God's presence. How can we incorporate prayerful reflection into our daily routines to deepen our relationship with God?

Reflection: *Reflect on Elijah's journey on Mount Horeb and how he found God in the quiet moments. Consider how you can implement practices of prayer, solitude, and reflection to strengthen your connection with God during your college years.*

Let us pray... Dear God, we are inspired by Elijah's encounter with You on Mount Horeb, where he found Your presence in the silence and sought Your guidance. As we navigate the challenges and joys of college life, grant us the wisdom to find moments of stillness, listen for Your voice, and create sacred spaces where we can connect with You. May our faith be renewed, and our purpose clarified as we seek Your presence in our journey. Amen.

REFLECTING ON RELATIONSHIPS

41

INVESTING IN FRIENDSHIPS

"A friend loves at all times, and a brother is born for a time of adversity."

– PROVERBS 17:17 (NIV)

As we journey through the chapters of life, one invaluable treasure we discover is friendship. These bonds, woven with care and strengthened by shared experiences, have the power to uplift, support, and bring joy to our lives. Today, we look into the importance of investing in friendships – ones that go beyond the surface and stand the test of time.

Consider this: a friendship is like a garden. To cultivate a thriving garden, you must invest time, effort, and attention. Similarly, nurturing friendships requires intentional care and consistent effort. However, too much attention and you begin to kill it, you must find the balance that works for each individual plant in your garden. Proverbs 17:17 reminds us that a true friend loves at all times, even during the storms of life.

How to nurture your friendships:

1. **Quality Time:** Spend quality time with your friends. Engage in meaningful conversations, share your thoughts and feelings, and truly listen when they speak. These moments of connection build trust and strengthen your bond.

2. **Consistency:** Like tending to a garden regularly, consistency is key. Check in on your friends, celebrate their successes, and offer support during challenges. Even a simple text or call can make a significant difference.

3. **Empathy:** Practice empathy. Try to understand your friends' perspectives, emotions, and struggles. Offering empathy demonstrates that you care deeply about their well-being.

4. **Forgiveness:** In every relationship, there may be moments of misunderstanding or conflict. Learn to forgive and seek reconciliation. A forgiving heart allows friendships to endure through trials.

5. **Celebrating Uniqueness:** Appreciate the uniqueness of each friend. Embrace their individuality, quirks, and differences. A diverse circle of friends enriches your life.

Investing in friendships enriches your life with companionship, support, and shared experiences. These connections become a source of strength during challenging times and a wellspring of joy during moments of celebration. You'll have the potential to form lifelong bonds with college friends, and enrich your understanding of the world with perspectives from different backgrounds.

Reflection: *Reflect on your closest friendships. How have you invested in these relationships, and what impact have they had on your life?*

Consider the qualities of a true friend mentioned in Proverbs 17:17. How can you embody these qualities in your friendships?

Think about a time when a friend's support made a significant difference in your life. What did you learn from that experience?

Let us pray... Dear God, I thank you for the gift of friendship and the bonds I've formed with others. Help me to invest in these relationships with genuine care and consistent effort. May I be a true friend who loves at all times, walking alongside my friends through every season of life. Amen.

42

SMALL ACTS OF KINDNESS

"Be kind and compassionate to one another"

– EPHESIANS 4:32 (NIV)

Imagine a typical college morning – the rush to classes, the looming deadlines, and the weight of expectations. Amid this chaos, a friend notices your exhaustion and offers you their favorite coffee, just the way you like it. It's a small gesture, but it changes the entire trajectory of your day. That simple act of kindness provides a ray of sunshine in the midst of your hectic schedule, reminding you that you're not alone in this journey.

Small acts of kindness have the power to make a significant impact on someone's day. It brightens our day, lifts our spirits, and reminds us of the beauty of human connection. This story illustrates why practicing kindness in our daily interactions is so good—it has the potential to create a ripple effect of positivity and warmth in our relationships and our college community.

In the small acts of kindness we practice, we discover the profound impact of compassion and the ability to create a positive atmosphere amidst the chaos of our daily lives, and draw others closer to the love of Christ.

Reflection: *Recall a recent moment when someone's act of kindness touched your heart. How did it make you feel, and how did it impact your day?*

How can you intentionally practice kindness to create a more positive and supportive environment?

When was the last time you did a small act of kindness? How can you do more in the future?

Let us pray... Dear God, I thank you for the reminder of the transformative power of kindness. Help me to be a beacon of light in the chaos of college life, showing compassion and extending grace to those around me. May my acts of kindness reflect Your love and draw others closer to You. Amen.

43

NAVIGATING CONFLICT

"Bear with each other and forgive one another if any of you has a grievance against someone. Forgive as the Lord forgave you."

– COLOSSIANS 3:13 (NIV)

During the stressful periods of college we can often find ourselves entangled in conflicts. These conflicts can emerge in our friendships, study groups, or even within ourselves. Today, we reflect on the inevitability of conflicts in relationships and how we can navigate them constructively, following the example of Christ's grace and love.

Consider a situation where you and a close friend have a disagreement. The tension between you grows, and you feel frustration building up. Instead of letting it escalate, you decide to have an open and honest conversation. You both express your feelings and perspectives while actively listening to each other. Through this Christ-like approach of humility and understanding, you find common ground and a resolution that strengthens your friendship.

In this story, we witness the constructive handling of conflict. It demonstrates that conflicts are a natural part of relationships, but they don't have to be destructive. By following the principles of kindness, compassion, and forgiveness, we can address conflicts in a way that nurtures understanding and unity.

Handling conflicts with grace is essential for several reasons:

1. **Strengthening Relationships:** Constructive conflict resolution strengthens relationships by promoting understanding and empathy.

2. **Personal Growth:** It fosters personal growth as we learn to empathize with others and consider different perspectives.

3. **Reflecting Christ's Love:** Approaching conflicts with Christ's love and forgiveness reflects our commitment to His teachings.

4. **Building Trust:** Resolving conflicts constructively builds trust and enhances communication.

Conflict is an unavoidable part of human relationships, but it doesn't have to be detrimental. By following the example of Christ's grace, we can navigate conflicts with kindness, compassion, and forgiveness. Through these actions, we not only resolve differences but also strengthen our bonds with others and deepen our connection with our Savior.

Reflection: *Think of a recent conflict you encountered. How did you handle it, and what were the results? Could you have approached it differently?*

How can you apply kindness, compassion, and forgiveness when faced with conflicts in your relationships?

Reflect on the importance of open communication in resolving conflicts. How can you improve your listening and communication skills to handle conflicts more constructively?

Let us pray... Dear God, I seek Your guidance in navigating conflicts with grace and love. Help me approach disagreements with kindness, compassion, and forgiveness, just as You have forgiven me. May conflicts be opportunities for growth and deeper connections with others. Amen.

44

EMBRACING DIVERSITY

"There is neither Jew nor Gentile, neither slave nor free, nor is there male and female, for you are all one in Christ Jesus."

– GALATIANS 3:28 (NIV)

One of the remarkable aspects of college life is the opportunity to connect with people from diverse backgrounds, cultures, and perspectives. These interactions can be enriching and transformative. Today, we reflect on the beauty of embracing diversity and how God's love transcends differences, deepening our relationships.

Imagine you're part of a group project with classmates from various countries and cultures. At first, it might seem challenging to understand each other's viewpoints. However, as you work together and share your unique insights, you begin to appreciate the richness that diversity brings. You realize that, despite your differences, you are all striving for the same goal. This experience not only strengthens your project but also fosters meaningful connections.

In this story, we witness the power of diversity to enrich relationships. It reminds us that, in Christ, we are all one, regardless of our backgrounds, and our shared humanity can unite us in beautiful ways.

Diversity is a gift that can enrich our lives and relationships. As we encounter people from various backgrounds, let us approach them with open hearts, recognizing the beauty in our differences. In doing so, we reflect God's love, which transcends all distinctions.

Reflection: *Think about a time when you connected with someone from a diverse background. How did it enrich your perspective or relationship?*

Consider the verse from Galatians 3:28. How can you live out the truth that, in Christ, we are all one, regardless of our differences?

Reflect on how embracing diversity can strengthen your relationships and personal growth during your college journey.

Let us pray... Dear God, thank You for the diversity of people You bring into my life. Help me to embrace and appreciate our differences, recognizing that we are all one in Christ. May Your love shine through our relationships and enrich my college experience. Amen.

45

ACTIVE LISTENING

___ / ___ / _____

"My dear brothers and sisters, take note of this: Everyone should be quick to listen, slow to speak, and slow to become angry."

– JAMES 1:19 (NIV)

Effective communication is the cornerstone of healthy relationships, and throughout life we often encounter situations where communication can make or break connections.

One of the key parts of strengthening bonds through communication is active listening and understanding.

Imagine you have a close friend who is going through a tough time. They confide in you about their challenges and fears. Instead of immediately offering solutions or advice, you choose to actively listen. You let them express their feelings and concerns without interruption. Your friend appreciates your empathetic ear, and in that moment of shared vulnerability, your bond deepens.

Here, we witness the power of active listening and understanding. It illustrates that sometimes, the most valuable thing we can offer in a relationship is our presence and willingness to listen. It's essential to remember the wisdom from James 1:19: "be quick to listen, slow to speak." By actively listening and seeking to understand others, we can strengthen our relationships.

Reflection: *Recall a time when someone truly listened to you and how it made you feel. What can you do to offer that gift of listening to others?*

Consider the verse from James 1:19. How can you apply it in your daily interactions with friends, classmates, and acquaintances?

Let us pray... Dear God, grant me the wisdom and humility to be a better listener and to seek understanding in my relationships. May my communication be a source of strength and empathy as I navigate college life. Amen.

46

DIGITAL CONNECTIONS

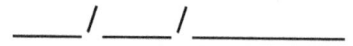

"As iron sharpens iron, so one person sharpens another."

– PROVERBS 27:17 (NIV)

In our digitally connected world, technology has revolutionized how we relate to one another. We use smartphones, social media, and messaging apps to connect with friends, both near and far.

While digital tools are incredibly useful for maintaining relationships and staying informed, we must also remember the profound value of face-to-face interactions. There's a unique depth and authenticity in sitting down with a friend, roommate, or classmate, engaging in meaningful conversation, and truly listening to one another. These in-person moments can be transformative. They allow us to share our joys and struggles, offer support, and build lasting bonds.

Balancing technology and meaningful relationships is essential for several reasons:

1. **Deepening Connections:** Face-to-face interactions foster deeper emotional bonds and understanding.

2. **Combatting Loneliness:** Meaningful in-person connections can combat the feelings of loneliness that can result from excessive digital interactions. Loneliness is a serious issue amongst men in the modern world so it's important to do everything we can to combat it.

3. **Enhancing Empathy:** Being physically present with someone allows us to pick up on nonverbal cues, enhancing our ability to empathize.

4. **Creating Memories:** Many of our most cherished memories are made during in-person experiences with friends and loved ones.

We are fortunate to live in a time when technology connects us with the world. However, let's remember the wisdom of Proverbs 27:17, which highlights the importance of people sharpening one another. Let's strive for a balance that allows us to harness the benefits of technology while also cultivating meaningful, face-to-face relationships that enrich our lives.

Reflection: *Think about your daily interactions. How do you balance digital connections with meaningful face-to-face relationships?*

Consider the verse from Proverbs 27:17. How can your relationships with others sharpen and enrich your life?

Reflect on the moments in college when face-to-face interactions have left a lasting impact on you.

Let us pray... Dear God, guide me in finding a healthy balance between digital connections and meaningful in-person relationships. May I cherish the beauty of face-to-face interactions as I navigate college life. Amen.

47

REMEMBERING CHRIST'S LOVE

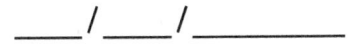

"A new command I give you: Love one another. As I have loved you, so you must love one another. By this, everyone will know that you are my disciples if you love one another."

– JOHN 13:34-35 (NIV)

Jesus' life was a living example of selfless love and sacrifice. He has taught us to love one another as He has loved us. Christ's love can serve us as a guiding light to help shape our interactions and relationships with others. It encourages us to be compassionate, empathetic, and caring toward others. It inspires us to build deeper connections, bridge gaps, and reconcile differences in our relationships.

John 13:34-35 reminds us that love is not just a feeling but an action. Let's strive to embody Christ's love in our interactions and relationships. Let's be the ones who extend a helping hand, offer encouragement, and show kindness to those around us. By doing so, you not only honor Christ's teachings but also create an atmosphere of love and unity in your community.

Reflection: *Think about a time when someone's act of love or kindness deeply impacted you. How did it make you feel, and how can you replicate that in your own interactions?*

Consider the people in your college life. How can you demonstrate Christ's love to them in practical ways?

Reflect on the verse from John 13:34-35. How does it guide your understanding of love and its role in your relationships?

Let us pray... Dear God, help me remember Christ's love as I navigate my relationships in college. May His example of selfless love inspire my interactions and guide me in building connections that reflect His teachings. Amen.

Bible Study - Learning from Jonathan and David

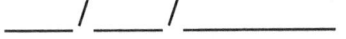

1 Samuel 18-20

The story of Jonathan and David in the Bible serves as a timeless example of the profound impact that strong, nurturing relationships can have on our lives. Just as their friendship was characterized by loyalty, support, and love, we can learn valuable lessons about how to foster and maintain meaningful relationships in our college years and beyond. This study will explore the enduring qualities of their friendship and how they can inspire us in our own relationships.

Reading: First, read the story of Jonathan and David in 1 Samuel 18-20 to gain insight into the qualities of their friendship.

Discussion Questions:

1. **Loyalty and Sacrifice**: Jonathan and David's friendship was marked by loyalty and a willingness to make sacrifices for each other. In what ways can loyalty and sacrifice strengthen our relationships with friends and loved ones?

2. **Mutual Support**: Throughout their friendship, Jonathan and David provided unwavering support to each other, even in challenging circumstances. How can we offer and seek support in our own relationships during both good and difficult times?

3. **Communication and Trust**: Effective communication and trust were essential in the relationship between Jonathan and David. How can open communication and trust be nurtured in our modern relationships, especially in an age of digital communication?

4. **Overcoming Challenges**: Jonathan and David faced obstacles and threats, yet their friendship endured. What lessons can we learn from their ability to overcome challenges in maintaining strong relationships?

5. **Friendship and Faith**: Jonathan and David's friendship was grounded in faith and trust in God. How can shared values and faith contribute to the depth of our own relationships?

6. **Long-lasting Impact**: The friendship of Jonathan and David left a lasting impact on both of their lives. How can we seek to create positive and enduring impacts on the lives of our friends and loved ones?

Reflection: *Reflect on the qualities of loyalty, support, and love exhibited by Jonathan and David in their friendship. Consider how these qualities can guide you in nurturing and maintaining strong relationships with those around you, especially during your college years.*

Let us pray... Dear God, we are inspired by the enduring friendship of Jonathan and David and the qualities of loyalty, support, and love they exemplified. As we seek to foster strong relationships in our own lives, grant us the wisdom to prioritize loyalty, offer unwavering support, and maintain open communication. May our friendships be a source of strength and encouragement, reflecting the love You have for each of us. Amen.

DIGITAL DETOX

49

DIGITAL DETOX

____ / ____ / _____

"He says, 'Be still, and know that I am God; I will be exalted among the nations, I will be exalted in the earth.'"

– PSALM 46:10 (NIV)

Have you ever took part in a digital detox?

Our lives are often filled with the constant buzz of electronic devices. Whether it's our smartphones, laptops, or tablets, the noise of technology can become overwhelming. It invades our personal space and can affect our sleep quality and overall well-being.

Psalm 46:10 reminds us to "be still and know that I am God." In a world filled with digital distractions, being still is a radical act of self-care. It's in these moments of stillness that we can reconnect with our faith, find peace, and regain a sense of balance.

Research has shown that excessive screen time before bedtime can disrupt our sleep patterns. The blue light emitted by screens can interfere with our body's production of melatonin, a hormone that regulates sleep. By setting a time in the evening to disconnect from electronic devices, we allow our minds and bodies to prepare for restful sleep, leading to improved overall well-being.

Reflection: *How often do you find yourself immersed in digital devices before bedtime? What impact does this have on your sleep and well-being?*

Reflect on a time when you intentionally disconnected from technology and experienced a sense of stillness and peace. What did you learn from that experience?

Consider setting a specific time in the evening for a digital detox. How can this practice benefit your sleep quality and overall well-being?

Let us pray... Dear God, in the midst of digital noise, help me find moments of stillness and connection with You. Grant me the wisdom to set aside electronic devices in the evening, allowing for better sleep and improved well-being. Thank You for the gift of stillness. Amen.

50

RESISTING THE FEAR OF MISSING OUT (FOMO)

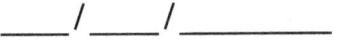

"There is a time for everything, and a season for every activity under the heavens."

– ECCLESIASTES 3:1 (NIV)

FOMO is a feeling we've all experienced. It's that nagging thought that there's something better happening elsewhere, that we're missing out on the "perfect" moment, or piece of information only found on social media. It's a powerful force that can lead us to spend countless hours scrolling through our screens trying to stay up-to-date with everything so we don't miss out on great content everyone else sees.

Ecclesiastes 3:1 reminds us that there is a time for everything. It's a reminder that each moment in our lives has its unique significance. When we're constantly on our phones, we miss the beauty of the present moment. Whether it's spending time with friends, studying, or simply enjoying solitude, each moment holds its own value.

Resisting FOMO doesn't mean disconnecting from the world entirely.

It means finding contentment in the activities and relationships that matter most to us. By being present in the moment, we can deepen our connections with others and create meaningful memories that won't be found on a screen.

Reflection: *Reflect on a time when you experienced FOMO. How did it affect your emotions and behavior?*

Consider the activities and relationships that bring you the most joy and fulfillment. How can you be more present in those moments?

Challenge yourself to spend a day without constantly checking your smartphone or social media. What did you discover about the present moment during that time?

Let us pray... Dear God, help me resist the grip of FOMO, which can steal away the joy of the present moment. Teach me to find contentment in the activities and relationships that matter most to me. Thank You for the gift of each moment. Amen.

51

MINDFUL SCREEN CONSUMPTION

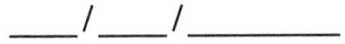

"I have the right to do anything," you say—but not everything is beneficial. "I have the right to do anything"—but I will not be mastered by anything."

- 1 CORINTHIANS 6:12 (NIV)

Many of us know the dangers of too much screentime, yet the majority of the population have excessive screentime anyway.

Screens offer us a wealth of information, entertainment, and connection, but they can also consume our time and attention. Mindful screen consumption involves recognizing the impact of our digital choices on our mental, emotional, and spiritual well-being.

Being mindful means making intentional choices about what we consume online. It involves asking ourselves whether the content we engage with aligns with our values, faith, and well-being. It's about finding a balance between staying informed and maintaining our peace.

Reflection: *Take a moment to reflect on your screen consumption habits. Are there times when you've felt that your screen time was excessive or* *harmful? What changes can you make to practice more mindful screen consumption?*

Check your phone and see how much time, on average, you spend on your phone each day. Are you happy with your results, or not? How many hours would you like to spend on your phone each day? What could you do with all the free time you'd save yourself by spending less time on your phone?

Let us pray... Dear God, guide me in my choices when it comes to screen consumption. Help me find a balance that aligns with my faith, values, and well-being. Let Your Word be the ultimate source of guidance in my life. Amen.

Rediscovering Face-to-Face Interaction

___/___/_____

"Two are better than one, because they have a good return for their labor: If either of them falls down, one can help the other up. But pity anyone who falls and has no one to help them up."

– Ecclesiastes 4:9-10 (NIV)

It seems as if genuine face-to-face interaction has become a rarity. Digital communication has its benefits, but it often lacks the depth and authenticity of face-to-face conversations. In-person interactions allow us to see and feel each other's emotions, creating a more profound connection and enabling us to better understand each other and support one another. When we engage in face-to-face conversations, we also practice active listening and empathy.

In a world where isolation and loneliness can creep in, spending time with friends, family, and fellow believers in real life can provide a sense of belonging and purpose. Ecclesiastes 4:9-10 reminds us that two are better than one. We are created for community, and face-to-face interactions are an essential part of building and nurturing relationships.

Reflection: *Take a moment to reflect on how often you engage in face-to-face conversations compared to digital interactions. Are there relationships in your life that could benefit from more in-person time?*

How can you push for more real-life connections rather than just digital ones?

Let us pray... Dear God, help me prioritize face-to-face interactions and nurture meaningful relationships. May I be present and attentive in my conversations, showing love and empathy to those around me. Thank you for the gift of genuine connections. Amen.

53

ANALOG HOBBIES

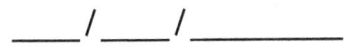

"The heavens declare the glory of God; the skies proclaim the work of his hands."

– PSALM 19:1 (NIV)

In today's fast-paced, digitally driven society, analog hobbies offer a respite. They allow us to disconnect from screens, slow down, and embrace simplicity.

Engaging in outdoor activities like rock climbing or hiking awakens your adventurous spirit. These offline activities provide an opportunity to explore the natural world, connect with others, and embrace the thrill of physical challenges.

Perhaps you aren't the physical type. In-person conventions and live performances provide unique opportunities to build meaningful connections. Meeting like-minded individuals and sharing experiences can foster friendships that last a lifetime.

Whatever it is you choose, analog hobbies encourage mindfulness and stress relief. At these moments you're taking part in the activities you're fully immersed in the moment, letting go of worries and distractions, and calming your mind.

Reflection: *When was the last time you engaged in an analog hobby like rock climbing, hiking, or attending a live event? How did it make you feel?*

Are there analog activities you used to enjoy but have neglected due to digital distractions?

How can you incorporate more analog hobbies into your daily life to find balance and promote well-being?

Let us pray... Dear God, I thank you for the gift of analog hobbies that allow me to disconnect from the digital noise and rediscover simplicity. Help me nurture my adventurous spirit, build meaningful connections, find mindful presence, and alleviate stress through these activities. Guide me in finding the right balance between the digital and analog worlds. Amen.

54

SUCCESS STORY

____/____/_____

"He says, 'Be still, and know that I am God; I will be exalted among the nations, I will be exalted in the earth.'"

– PSALM 46:10 (NIV)

Let's explore the journey of Mason, a college student who, like many of us, was ensnared by the grip of screens, experienced profound loneliness and anxiety, but ultimately discovered transformation, improved mental and emotional health, and a newfound sense of purpose.

Mason's screen time was consuming his life. Constant scrolling had replaced genuine connections, leaving him feeling isolated and overwhelmed. The illusion of social media had fueled his anxiety, making him compare his life to carefully curated online personas.

One day, Mason decided he couldn't go on like this. He took a bold step and deleted his social media apps. The initial days were a struggle. He felt a void, an emptiness that seemed insurmountable. Loneliness crept in even stronger.

But, slowly, Mason's life began to change. With his screens set aside, he decided to reach out to old friends and initiate meaningful conversations. The more he engaged in face-to-face interactions, the less lonely he felt.

As Mason practiced mindfulness, he discovered the power of silence. He began meditating, journaling his thoughts and emotions, and spending time in nature. The silence he once feared became a sanctuary of self-discovery.

Without the constant digital distractions, Mason found a renewed sense of purpose. He began volunteering, attending local events, and dedicating time to hobbies he'd neglected. The emptiness was gradually replaced with fulfillment.

Mason's transformation was profound. He went from feeling profoundly lonely and anxious to experiencing inner peace and joy. Unplugging allowed him to "be still" as Psalm 46:10 suggests and recognize God's presence in the silence.

Reflection: *Have you ever experienced feelings of loneliness or anxiety due to excessive screen time?*

Can you relate to Mason's journey from isolation to meaningful connections?

How can you incorporate mindfulness and unplugging into your life to discover purpose, joy, and peace?

Let us pray... Dear God, I pray for the courage to unplug from screens when needed and rediscover the joy and peace that comes from connecting with You, others, and myself. Help me find balance in this digital age and use technology as a tool for growth and connection. Amen.

Bible Study - Restoring the Temple

___ / ___ / _____

2 Chronicles 29-30

The story of the cleansing and rededication of the temple in 2 Chronicles 29-30 offers a powerful biblical parallel to the theme of digital detox. Just as King Hezekiah sought to restore the temple to its original purpose and holiness, we, too, can strive to cleanse our lives from the distractions of the digital world and rededicate ourselves to a life of greater focus, mindfulness, and purpose.

Reading: First, read 2 Chronicles 29-30 to gain insight into the temple's cleansing and rededication.

Discussion:

1. **The Temple Cleansing**: In 2 Chronicles 29, King Hezekiah initiated the cleansing of the temple. What motivated him to take this action, and how does it relate to the need for a digital detox in our lives?

2. **Removing Impurities**: The temple cleansing involved removing impurities and restoring the sacred space. What are some digital "impurities" or distractions in your life that might hinder your spiritual or personal growth?

3. **Renewal and Rededication**: The rededication of the temple in 2 Chronicles 29-30 was a time of renewal and commitment to God. How can a digital detox serve as a time of renewal for our relationship with God and our priorities?

4. **Community and Unity**: Hezekiah invited the entire community to participate in the rededication, fostering unity and communal worship. How can we involve our communities or friends in a digital detox to encourage one another in maintaining a healthy balance?

5. **Repentance and Forgiveness**: The Israelites sought God's forgiveness during this process. In what ways can a digital detox be an opportunity for reflection, repentance, and seeking God's guidance in our lives?

6. **Balanced Technology Use**: How can we establish a balanced approach to technology in our daily lives, ensuring it serves as a tool for productivity, connection, and learning rather than a

distraction?

Reflection: *Consider the lessons from the temple cleansing and rededication in 2 Chronicles 29-30 and apply them to your own life. Reflect on the impurities you may need to remove from your digital habits and how rededicating your time and focus to God can lead to a healthier relationship with technology.*

Let us pray... Dear God, we thank You for the lessons from the cleansing and rededication of the temple in 2 Chronicles. As we strive to find a balanced relationship with technology, guide us in identifying and removing digital impurities from our lives. May our digital detox be a time of renewal, reflection, and a deeper connection with You. Grant us the wisdom to maintain a healthy balance in our use of technology. Amen.

DREAMS AND ASPIRATIONS

56

GOD'S UNIQUE PLAN

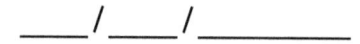

"For I know the plans I have for you, declares the LORD, plans for welfare and not for evil, to give you a future and a hope."

– JEREMIAH 29:11

As we journey into the final chapter of your evening devotional, I want to talk about something that's been on my heart - God's unique plan for each of us. You see, I've been where you are, navigating the exciting yet often uncertain path of college life. And just like you, I had dreams and aspirations, goals I wanted to achieve, and a future I hoped to build.

But here's the thing: sometimes, we can get so caught up in our own plans that we forget about God's plan for us. Jeremiah 29:11 reminds us that God has plans for us, and they are plans for our welfare, not harm. Plans that give us a future filled with hope. It's like having the best GPS system for life.

When I was in college, I had a dream of pursuing a particular career path. I was so focused on my vision that I didn't always consider what God might have in store for me. But as I journeyed through those years, I encountered unexpected opportunities and challenges that reshaped my direction.

God's unique plan for each of us is like a masterpiece, intricately woven with purpose and filled with adventures we might not have anticipated. Embracing God's plan doesn't mean giving up on your dreams; it means aligning your dreams with His divine purpose.

Reflection: *Are you so fixated on your own plans that you might be missing out on what God has in store for you?*

Can you recall a time when an unexpected turn in your college journey led to something positive?

How can you seek and discern God's unique plan for your life, especially during your college years?

Let us pray... Dear God, as I stand on the threshold of my college years, help me to trust in Your unique plan for my life. Keep my heart open to Your guidance and my dreams aligned with Your purpose. Give me the wisdom to recognize Your hand in the unexpected twists and turns of my journey. Amen.

Chasing Your Dreams

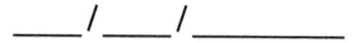

"Trust in the Lord with all your heart and lean not on your own understanding; in all your ways submit to him, and he will make your paths straight."

– Proverbs 3:5-6 (NIV)

If you're serious about chasing your dreams, it's essential you do so with faith and determination. To do this, we can take inspiration from the stories of Joseph and Daniel.

Think about Joseph. He had dreams of greatness, but his path was filled with adversity. He faced betrayal by his own brothers, was sold into slavery, and was unjustly imprisoned. But through it all, Joseph remained faithful to God. In the end, he became a powerful leader and fulfilled the dreams God had given him.

Now, let's consider Daniel. He was taken from his homeland to serve in a foreign king's court. Despite facing the temptation to compromise his faith, Daniel remained steadfast in his devotion to God. This unwavering faith not only saved his life in the lion's den but also allowed him to thrive in a foreign land.

The common thread in these stories is faith—faith in God's plan and His timing. As you pursue your dreams in college, you will encounter obstacles, setbacks, and moments of doubt. But like Joseph and Daniel, you can overcome them with faith in the God who knows your path.

Don't be discouraged by the challenges you face. Instead, embrace them as opportunities to help achieve your dreams. Trust that God has a unique plan for your life, and even when things seem uncertain, He is guiding your steps.

Reflection: *Are there dreams and aspirations you're currently pursuing or hope to pursue in college? What challenges or obstacles do you anticipate or have already encountered?*

How can you apply the lessons of faith and determination from the stories of Joseph and Daniel to your own life and dreams?

Take a moment to pray and commit your dreams and aspirations to God, asking for His guidance and strength to pursue them with faith.

Let us pray... Dear God, as I pursue my dreams in college, I'm inspired by the faith of Joseph and Daniel. Help me trust Your plan and remain determined through challenges. Guide me and lead me in Your wisdom. I surrender my aspirations to Your capable hands. Amen.

FACING SETBACKS

"And we know that in all things God works for the good of those who love him, who have been called according to his purpose."

- ROMANS 8:28 (NIV)

As you chase your dreams and aspirations in college, you'll undoubtedly encounter moments of setbacks and disappointments. These setbacks are not meant to break you but to shape you into the person God envisions you to be.

A friend of mine from college, Anthony, was an exceptional student with a dream of becoming a successful entrepreneur. He launched his first business during his sophomore year, pouring his heart and soul into it. Everything seemed promising, but one day, a major financial setback hit him like a ton of bricks.

The business faced unexpected challenges, leading to financial losses and a sense of failure. He felt defeated, questioning whether he was on the right path. He even considered giving up on his dream.

During this time, Anthony clung to Romans 8:28, "And we know that in all things God works for the good of those who love him, who have been called according to his purpose." He began to see his setback as an opportunity for growth, not a roadblock.

He learned that setbacks are a part of the journey, not the end of it. They can refine your character, teach resilience, and deepen your faith. By persevering through adversity, he discovered strengths within himself that he didn't know existed.

As you face setbacks, remember that God is always at work behind the scenes. Perhaps these setbacks are guiding you toward a more refined dream or revealing new talents you never knew you had.

In the face of adversity, hold on to your faith. Trust that God is using these challenges to prepare you for a brighter future. Embrace setbacks as stepping stones toward your dreams, for His plans for you are far greater than you can imagine.

Reflection: *Have you experienced a setback or disappointment recently? How did it make you feel?*

Can you think of a time when a setback led to a positive outcome or personal growth?

How can you apply Romans 8:28 to your life when facing adversity?

Let us pray... Dear God, in moments of setbacks and disappointments, help me to trust in Your greater plan for my life. Grant me the faith to see beyond my present circumstances and the determination to press on toward my dreams. May I find strength and growth in adversity, knowing that You are always with me, working for my good. Amen.

59

FEAR OF FAILURE

___/___/_____

"Have I not commanded you? Be strong and courageous. Do not be afraid; do not be discouraged, for the LORD your God will be with you wherever you go."

- JOSHUA 1:9 (NIV)

One of the most common obstacles on the path to realizing your dreams is the fear of failure. It's that nagging voice that whispers, "What if you're not good enough?" or "What if you don't succeed?"

Consider the story of Peter, one of Jesus' disciples. Peter had a dream of walking on water, but when he stepped out of the boat onto the stormy sea, fear overwhelmed him, and he began to sink. In that moment, he doubted his abilities and feared failure.

Similarly, many of you might hesitate to chase your dreams because of the fear of falling short. You might think, "What if I don't get that internship I applied for?" or "What if my startup idea doesn't take off?"

It's essential to recognize that fear of failure is a common human experience. However, it's also an opportunity for growth. God's message to Joshua in Joshua 1:9 applies to you as well: "Have I not commanded you?

Be strong and courageous. Do not be afraid; do not be discouraged, for the LORD your God will be with you wherever you go."

Failure doesn't define your worth. It's merely a step in your journey towards success. If Peter had allowed fear to stop him from stepping out of the boat, he would never have experienced the miracle of walking on water.

Remember, many of the world's most successful individuals faced repeated failures on their journey to greatness. Walt Disney faced multiple business failures before creating Disneyland. Steve Jobs was fired from his own company, Apple, before returning to revolutionize the tech industry.

Your dreams are worth pursuing. Don't let the fear of failure paralyze you. Instead, see it as a stepping stone, a chance to learn, adapt, and grow stronger. Know that God is with you in every step of your journey, even when you stumble. Trust that, just like Peter, you can rise above your fears and achieve remarkable things.

Reflection: *Can you think of a dream you've hesitated to pursue due to fear of failure? What holds you back?*

Reflect on a time when you faced failure or a setback. What did you learn from that experience?

How can you apply Joshua 1:9 to overcome your fear of failure and pursue your dreams with confidence?

Let us pray... Dear God, I confess that the fear of failure often holds me back from pursuing my dreams. Help me to remember Your promise to be with me wherever I go. Grant me the strength and courage to face my fears, embrace failures as opportunities for growth, and chase my dreams with confidence. Let Your presence be my source of strength. Amen.

60

Perseverance and Patience

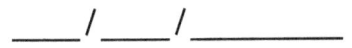

"Let us not become weary in doing good, for at the proper time we will reap a harvest if we do not give up."

- Galatians 6:9 (NIV)

As you pursue your dreams, your perseverance and patience are going to be tested. Sometimes, it will feel like you're sowing seeds in barren soil, and you may wonder if your efforts will ever bear fruit.

Do you know the story of the parable of the sower? In this story, a farmer scatters seeds, and they fall on different types of soil. Some seeds wither away, some are choked by thorns, but some fall on fertile ground and produce a bountiful harvest.

Your dreams are like those seeds. The journey to achieving them can be long and challenging, filled with obstacles and setbacks. It's easy to become discouraged, especially when you face rejection or when results don't come as quickly as you'd like.

But Galatians 6:9 reminds us, "Let us not become weary in doing good, for at the proper time we will reap a harvest if we do not give up."

Imagine the perseverance of the farmer. Despite challenges, he keeps sowing, nurturing, and patiently waiting for the harvest. Similarly, your dreams require dedication, continuous effort, and faith in God's timing.

Think of famous authors like J.K. Rowling, who faced multiple rejections before Harry Potter became a phenomenon. Or scientists like Thomas Edison, who famously said, "I have not failed. I've just found 10,000 ways that won't work."

Your dreams may not come to fruition overnight, but remember that it's the process of sowing, nurturing, and patiently waiting that strengthens your character and faith. Each setback is an opportunity to learn and grow.

As you persevere and exercise patience, you'll discover the incredible resilience within you. Like the seeds that found fertile ground, your dreams will take root and eventually flourish.

So, embrace perseverance and patience as companions on your journey. Keep sowing your seeds, tending to them with diligence, and trust that in God's perfect timing, you will reap a bountiful harvest.

Reflection: *Are there dreams or goals you've considered giving up on due to impatience or discouragement?*

Reflect on a time when perseverance led to success in your life or someone else's.

How can you apply the principles of Galatians 6:9 to your pursuit of dreams?

Let us pray... Dear God, I often grow weary when chasing my dreams, especially when faced with setbacks and delays. Help me to remember the importance of perseverance and patience. Grant me the strength to keep sowing, nurturing, and waiting for the harvest, trusting in Your perfect timing. May I find resilience in the process and grow closer to You through it. Amen.

61

LEGACY AND IMPACT

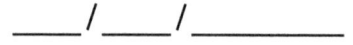

"And whatever you do, whether in word or deed, do it all in the name of the Lord Jesus, giving thanks to God the Father through him."

- COLOSSIANS 3:17 (NIV)

While you pursue your dreams and aspirations, it's important to reflect on the legacy you desire to leave behind. What kind of impact do you hope to make on your community and the world around you?

In Colossians 3:17, we are reminded, "And whatever you do, whether in word or deed, do it all in the name of the Lord Jesus, giving thanks to God the Father through him." This verse teaches us that every action, every pursuit, and every dream can become an opportunity to glorify God and leave a lasting, positive legacy.

Think about some of the great individuals who have left enduring legacies. People like Martin Luther King Jr., who dreamed of a world free from racial injustice, and Mother Teresa, whose selfless service to the poor continues to inspire generations. Their dreams and actions were fueled by a desire to make the world a better place.

Your dreams, whether they are in academics, career, or service, have the potential to create a ripple effect of positive change. It might be through groundbreaking research, compassionate leadership, or acts of kindness that touch the lives of others.

Consider this: What values, principles, and qualities do you want to be known for? How can your dreams and aspirations align with these ideals to create a legacy of significance?

Perhaps your dream is to excel in your chosen field, influencing others by your dedication and integrity. Or maybe it's to be a source of encouragement and support for those in need. Whatever it may be, remember that your dreams can have a profound impact.

As you reflect on your legacy, think about the lives you can touch and the difference you can make. Embrace your dreams as a means to serve others, honoring God through your actions.

It's easy to become preoccupied with personal success, but true fulfillment comes when you use your gifts and aspirations to bless others. By pursuing your dreams with a servant's heart, you can leave a legacy that reflects God's love and grace.

So, dream boldly and chase your aspirations with dedication, knowing that your legacy will be a testament to God's goodness and the positive impact you've had on the lives of those around you.

Reflection: *What legacy would you like to leave behind in your community or the world?*

How can you align your dreams and aspirations with values and principles that reflect God's love?

Think about someone whose legacy has inspired you. What qualities or actions of theirs do you admire and want to emulate?

Let us pray... Dear God, I thank You for the dreams and aspirations You've placed in my heart. Help me to pursue them with purpose and dedication, always mindful of the legacy I wish to leave behind. May my actions and endeavors bring honor to Your name and be a source of blessing to others. Guide me in using my gifts and dreams to make a positive impact on my community and the world. Amen.

Bible Study - Joseph: From Dreamer to Ruler

Genesis 37-50

Joseph's story in the Book of Genesis (chapters 37-50) is a remarkable journey of faith, resilience, and the pursuit of dreams. As a young dreamer, he faced the challenges of betrayal, adversity, and imprisonment. However, through God's guidance and Joseph's unwavering faith, he ultimately rose to become a ruler in Egypt, second only to Pharaoh. This study will delve into Joseph's experiences and draw valuable lessons on persevering through challenges and setbacks as you chase your dreams.

Reading: First read Genesis 37-50 to immerse yourself in Joseph's incredible story.

Discussion Questions:

1. **Dreams and Aspirations**: Joseph had dreams early in his life that indicated his future leadership. Have you ever had a dream or aspiration that seemed challenging or distant? What was it, and how did you react to it initially?

2. **Betrayal and Resilience**: Joseph faced betrayal by his own brothers, who sold him into slavery. How do you think he managed to maintain his faith and resilience despite this adversity? What can you learn from his response to betrayal?

3. **Integrity in Adversity**: Throughout his life, Joseph consistently upheld his integrity and moral values, even when facing temptation. Can you recall a situation where you had to make a difficult moral choice? How did Joseph's example inspire you?

4. **Forgiveness and Reconciliation**: Joseph's eventual reconciliation with his brothers is a powerful example of forgiveness. Is there someone in your life whom you need to forgive or seek reconciliation with? How can Joseph's story guide you in this aspect?

5. **God's Providential Plan**: Joseph recognized God's providence throughout his life, even in the darkest moments. Have you ever experienced a situation where, in hindsight, you saw God's guidance or purpose? How did it affect your perspective on challenges?

6. **Perseverance and Achieving Dreams**: Joseph's journey was marked by perseverance, from being a slave to becoming a ruler.

How can you apply the lessons of Joseph's perseverance to your own dreams and aspirations?

7. **Support and Mentorship**: Joseph had unique relationships with individuals like Potiphar, the prison keeper, and Pharaoh. How can seeking support and mentorship from others help you on your journey toward your dreams?

Reflection: *Consider Joseph's journey in light of your own dreams and aspirations. Reflect on the challenges you may face and how Joseph's story can inspire you to persevere, maintain your integrity, and trust in God's plan.*

Let us pray... Dear God, we thank You for the inspiring story of Joseph and his journey from a dreamer to a ruler. Help us to apply the lessons of faith, resilience, and integrity in our pursuit of dreams and aspirations. Guide us through challenges and setbacks, just as You guided Joseph, and may our lives bring honor to Your name. Amen.

The Afterword

Congratulations on reaching the end of this book! I sincerely hope that it has been a valuable companion on your college journey. As you reflect on the pages you've read, I encourage you to take a moment to pause and contemplate the lessons you've learned, the wisdom you've gained, and the growth you've experienced.

Remember, the college years are just the beginning of a lifelong adventure. The knowledge and insights you've acquired here will serve as a foundation for your future endeavors. As you move forward, embrace the opportunities and challenges that await you, knowing that you are equipped with the tools to navigate them with confidence and purpose.

I want to express my deepest gratitude to you for choosing this book and allowing me to be a part of your college experience. As a self-publisher, every reader's support means the world to me. Your engagement with the content and your willingness to learn from my experiences reaffirm my purpose in sharing these words.

If you found this book valuable and impactful, I kindly ask for your support by leaving a review. Reviews play a crucial role in helping self-published authors like myself reach a wider audience. Your review will help other college students to benefit from this book!

You can do this by scanning the QR code below or by searching for "Biblical Teachings" on Amazon. Want further insights and teachings to deepen your faith and personal growth? Check out our other books!

Thank you once again for your readership, and may your college years continue to be filled with growth, joy, and endless possibilities!

www.ingramcontent.com/pod-product-compliance
Lightning Source LLC
Chambersburg PA
CBHW071206070526
44584CB00019B/2940